The Keys to Senior Housing

A Guide for Two Generations

Roberta Schultz Benor

PublishAmerica
Baltimore

© 2009 by Roberta Schultz Benor.
All rights reserved. No part of this book may be reproduced, stored in a retrieval system or transmitted in any form or by any means without the prior written permission of the publishers, except by a reviewer who may quote brief passages in a review to be printed in a newspaper, magazine or journal.

First printing

PublishAmerica has allowed this work to remain exactly as the author intended, verbatim, without editorial input.

Hardcover 978-1-4489-0332-0
Softcover 978-1-60749-025-8
PAperback 978-1-4512-4634-6
PUBLISHED BY PUBLISHAMERICA, LLLP
www.publishamerica.com
Baltimore

Printed in the United States of America

To David
with whom I am growing old

Contents

Chapter 1: Introduction 11
    The Perfect Solution to the Dilemma of Senior Housing 11
    Definition of Senior Housing 12
    Dignity and Independence 13
    What to Do with Your Keys 14
    My Professional and Personal Experience with Senior Housing . 15

Chapter 2: Making the Decision to Move
    "I'm Not Ready" 18
    Re-Defining Your Independence 18
    You Are the Star, but You Now Have a Director 19
    Applying Your Advice to Yourself 21
    Ah, Your Aging Parents 22
    Food for the Sandwich Generation 28
    Mental Inventory of Your Living Situation 32
    Senior Housing Test 32
        Part A—for Seniors 32
        Part B—for Adult Children 33
    Keys for Seniors 34
    Keys for Adult Children 35

Chapter 3: Doing the Homework
    "I Don't Want to Move to a Nursing Home" 37
    Professional Assessment 38
    Family Dynamics like "Goldilocks and the Three Bears" 38

Thinking About Living and Dying 39
Not in the Dark Test 40
Rules for the Conversation and Active Listening 41
Seven Topics for the Necessary Conversation Led by the Parent .. 42
Seven Topics for the Necessary Conversation Led by the Adult Child 43
Financial and Health Concerns 43
Power of Attorney, Living Will, Durable Power of Attorney for Health 45
Financial Records 48
Health Care and Insurance 49
Adult Protective Services 51
Two Daughters Talking on an Airplane to Miami 52
Where to Turn 55
Government Resources and Other Programs 56
Keys for Seniors 59
Keys for Adult Children 60

Chapter 4: Learning About the Housing Options

"I'm Not Sure" 61
Aging in Place 61
    Making Your Home Safe 62
    Assistive Devices 63
    Driving or Not 65
    Proper Nutrition 66
    Home Care 66
    Managing Care from a Distance 68
    Being a Caregiver 68
    Guilt and Siblings 69

Moving in with Family 71
    Dealing with Giving Care 72
    Keeping Other Family Members Informed 74
    Hiring a Senior Aide 75
Adult Day Care 76
Congregate Housing 78
Group Home or Compound 80
Naturally Occurring Retirement Community (NORC) 81
Continuing Care Retirement Community (CCRC) 83
Independent Living 84
Assisted Living 87
Nursing Home 88
Hospice 91
Keys for Seniors 93
Keys for Adult Children 93

Chapter 5: Having the Interview
"I Don't Know" 94
Ways Interviews Should Be Conducted 95
Anxiety, Anger, and Excitement 99
Eighteen Questions You Should Ask at the Interview 100
What Your Answers Should Be 101
How the Interviews Should Not Go 103
Keys for Seniors 105
Keys for Adult Children 106

Chapter 6: Downsizing

"I Don't Have a Clue" 107
    The Big Six Downsizing Questions 107
    Dividing Up the Moving Tasks 108
    A Time for Introspection 108
    Frustration and Patience 110
    Grieving About Moving 111
    Deciding What to Take 112
    Saving a Special Object from Each Room 115
    Having a Closure Ceremony 115
    Family Involvement and Notifications 116
    Keys for Seniors 118
    Keys for Adult Children 119

Chapter 7: Moving In

"I Don't Remember" 120
    First Observations 121
    Family as Worker Bees and Parent as Queen Bee ... 121
    Mind and Body Workouts After Moving 124
    Taking Some R and R: Rest and Regrouping 124
    Laughing at the Mess Around You and the Mess in Your Head 125
    Learning About the New Place 126
    Developing Friendships 129
    Successful Staff 129
    Understanding Concepts of Aging 132
    Communal Meals 132
    Exceeding Expectations 134
    Keys for Seniors 138
    Keys for Adult Children 139

Chapter 8: Acclimating

"I Love It Here" 140

Coming Together 140

Enlarging Upon Your Lifestyle 143

Trying the Good and the Bad 145

Home with the Range of People 146

Voices Are Heard 148

Interacting 152

Conversation Icebreakers 153

Range of Activities 155

Being Part of the Community 157

Touching Base with Your Director 158

"Reinforcing Dignity in a Well-Elderly HUD Residence" 160

Keys for Seniors 167

Keys for Adult Children 168

Chapter 9: Conclusion 169

Is This Your Last Address? 169

Future Possibilities 170

Final Thoughts 171

Chapter 10: Resources 174

Chapter 1
Introduction

The Perfect Solution to the Dilemma of Senior Housing

I have the perfect solution to the dilemma of senior housing: do something. Saying you will decide at a later time may limit your options. Do something sooner rather than later. It is better that you assess your current living situation now and study your options. You want to do all this before your health deteriorates or before your family stages an intervention to get you out of an unhealthy or unsafe environment. This book will explain to seniors and adult children how to make the decisions related either to staying in the current home with modifications or to moving to an appropriate senior facility. For those family members who are dealing with your aging parents, you will learn here how you can help to direct your parent into living in the best kind of senior housing for this phase or the next phase of his life.

Definition of Senior Housing

What is senior housing? It is a place where seniors live, ranging from aging in your own residence to different kinds of group settings that meet your physical and mental needs. Some of those living facilities are your own home, the home of a relative, a congregate housing service, a group home or compound, an independent living community, a naturally occurring retirement community, a continuing care retirement community, an assisted living place, a nursing home, or a hospice service or center.

To the adult child, I say maybe your parent is doing fine where he lives. Then these are the easy years for you. Savor them, but please realize that your parent's physical or mental health will change, probably making the place where he now lives no longer suitable. I caution you to take this time to learn about what housing is available for the various phases through which your parent probably will journey. However, knowing the kinds of facilities that exist is only part of the issue. You also want to be confident in having the necessary skills to approach your parent who might be afraid to move or who does not think there is anything wrong with where or how he lives. You want to balance respect for your parent with the reality of his changing situation. If there are other siblings and relatives invested in this matter, then you will have to consider their concerns.

I am addressing both age groups in plain sight of each

other, so everyone can understand the issues that the different generations are facing. Throughout the book, I fluctuate in talking to each group, because the issues involve both ages. Also, before you know it, you adult children will be the elders thinking about your own appropriate senior housing. I offer these guideposts to help all of you deal with the challenges of maintaining or seeking a safe living environment.

Dignity and Independence

To the seniors, I ask you what you most want in your remaining years. The majority of you would probably answer that you want your dignity and your independence. I would say that dignity is your self-respect, and no one can take that from you, because it comes from within you. However, independence comes from your relationships to those outside of you and may have to be lessened or modified to grant you the most safe environment. Some of the *Webster's Dictionary* definitions of independent are "not dependent, not subject to control by others, not requiring or relying on others as for care or livelihood." When you have reached the point in your life when you or someone else feels that a change needs to be made in your living situation, it is time to re-define your independence. You are really not totally independent. I am really not totally independent. No one really is. So what is the definition with which you can live now? Having your independence is indicating your desire for as much freedom as health and safety will now allow.

If you are managing where you are now and your loved ones agree, please remember that someone once said that "managing" looks like it is a compound word of "man aging." So the more you age, the more you have to take stock of your situation and make sure it is the safest and healthiest for you. But it is wise to anticipate the next steps in that aging process and to prepare for dealing with those impending changes.

What to Do with Your Keys

The classic example of getting old and having a declining memory revolves around losing one's keys. For those of us who have spent time searching for them, we come to the realization that we should be more organized and put the keys in the same place each time. I am offering you a way to restructure your thought process regarding your senior housing choices, so that when you are presented with actual new keys or the symbolic key of crossing the threshold to a new place, you will feel as though you are organized, that you are in control of your situation within new boundaries. By learning about these topics of modifying your current home or of making the decision to move, doing the homework, learning about the choices, having the interview, downsizing, moving in, and acclimating, you will have the keys to successful senior living. I want you to have a conversation that flows from

"I'm not ready" to "I don't want to move to a nursing home" to "I'm not sure" to "I don't know" to "I don't have a clue" to "I don't remember" to the realization of "I love it here."

You might feel better about your aging situation if you realize that these majestic ideas from "Ulysses" by Alfred, Lord Tennyson can apply to you now:

> Tho' much is taken, much abides; and tho'
> We are not now that strength which in old days
> Moved earth and heaven; that which we are, we are;
> One equal temper of heroic hearts,
> Made weak by time and fate, but strong in will
> To strive, to seek, to find, and not to yield.

So you are not what you used to be, but you or your family member or both of you together must take the time now to strive, to seek, to find the best place for you to live. It may be your current home or it may be a facility with more care options for you. Please remember that your adult children want you to be safe and happy.

My Professional and Personal Experience with Senior Housing

I have had thirteen years of professional experience and several decades of personal experience with my mother-in-law living with us and my parents moving to an independent living facility. My familiarity with lifestyle change and with the types of senior housing enables me to provide to you a way of addressing your living situation. I have the keys to your new address in senior living and will now share them with you. In my professional years as activities coordinator, director of resident services, and then director of Filbert Gardens, I conducted 694 interviews with potential residents. About a third were not interested in moving there, about a third did not meet the criteria for moving in and were deleted from our list, and about a third did move in.

The anecdotes I use are here to make a point or to teach a lesson, but I have changed the details relating to these people to protect their privacy or have made up composites to illustrate examples from real people and real experiences I have had. Filbert Gardens is a fictitious name of a place based on the subsidized senior citizen high-rise where I was employed. My enjoyment of working there and any success I had are due in large part to an outstanding staff, board of directors, management company, supervisors, family support groups, and residents whose average age was 83. The specific procedures and activities at Filbert Gardens worked well at this independent living building, but many of the same things can be duplicated or modified for use in congregate housing services, group homes or compounds, naturally occurring retirement communities, continuing care retirement communities, assisted living facilities and nursing homes. So when you read of what happened at Filbert Gardens, know that in your senior housing facility, you can now have the benefits of these lessons.

When I personally arrive at the chronological or physical time that requires me to modify my home and to seek extra help to deal with my aging or illness, I will adjust. When I reach the next stage that tells me I should move, I will be scared and worried, but I do plan to move to the appropriate type of senior facility. I feel that the benefits of community and safety make it an excellent choice for prolonging health and happiness.

Based on my professional and personal experience, I have listed the "keys" for both age groups, the seniors and their families, at the ends of the next chapters. I hope that these keys will open your minds and your relationships to enable you to live successfully throughout your senior years.

Chapter 2
Making the Decision to Move

"I'm Not Ready"

I am going to give you the answer first, then the question. Answer: "It may be time for you to re-define your independence." Question: "Why do I have to give up my independence?" You are not giving it up completely, but you may have to modify it so your environment is safer. That may mean that you have to make changes in your current place or that you should move to another type of housing. But at each step of the journey, you will be making your own decisions within new parameters, maybe of your own choosing or maybe ones thrust upon you because of your changing health and abilities.

Re-Defining Your Independence

It may be that in your family, both generations, the seniors and their adult children, have come to a point where the aging process has created challenges for them personally or for their loved ones. You may feel that there is nothing wrong, but your children may feel worried about your current living conditions. You do not want to give up your independence, but my point is that you are not giving it up completely. You may still be able to live on your own, but you may now need to have more help in areas of personal hygiene, nutrition, financial management, and medication administration.

Or it may be time for you to move. It could be that in other periods of your life, you moved without much effort. Maybe the reason for prior moves was to go to school, to start a new job, to get married, or to retire. But all of a sudden, as the calendar pages turn faster and faster without your controlling them, the thought of moving may seem daunting, overwhelming, demoralizing, and intimidating. So the more homework you do, the more you study options available for you, and the more you involve your relatives and friends in the process, the smoother the transition should be.

You Are the Star, but You Now Have a Director

For these last scenes of your life, and may there be many as you continue your aging process, you are the star, but others around you may now have to be the director, guiding you to a suitable housing setting.

At every age, we want to be independent. It is natural to do what we can to grow up and live independently. The toddler says that she wants to put on her sweater "by myself!" The child says that he wants to walk to the school bus "alone." The teenager demands to be on the computer "without supervision." The newlywed wants to live her life "as she wants." The recent parent wants to raise his children "without interference." The retiree wants to revel in "time on his own." These are normal feelings: by myself, alone, without supervision, as you want, without interference, and time on your own.

However, the time comes when you do need more help to manage in the course of everyday life. If you are able to ask for the help or get it on your own, that is excellent. The more problematic part comes when others around you know it is time for you to have more help and you do not agree. Try to view your situation from the outside for a moment. If you heard a story about one of your friends who was living in an unsafe home, or was forgetting to take his medicine, or was driving when she should no longer be, what would you counsel that person? Or what would you think privately? You should reason that it is time for that person to re-define independence, meaning that a person can make decisions on his own, but he now needs certain parameters or limits on how he can make those decisions. For example, his limited independence may mean that he can walk to the store, but he has to use a cane so he will not fall. Or that he may stay in his home, but he has to install a chair lift to get him to his bedroom upstairs. Or that he might need to move to an assisted living building but he makes the decision as to which place it will be.

Applying Your Advice to Yourself

So maybe you should now apply that advice to yourself. You should not wait until after a stroke or heart attack to make such life-changing decisions. You should have a plan of what you will do at each stage of your senior life. You are not giving up your independence completely. You are actually re-defining it to make your life safer and easier.

If you do not have children or your relationship with them is beyond repair, I would hope that you can designate a friend or other relative to be your helper in this time of re-defining your independence and of supporting you though the decision-making process. Another alternative would be to appoint an attorney or a geriatric case manager or geriatric care manager to work on your behalf. The important thing is to have these discussions with someone who can help you see your situation through other eyes and can help you make decisions so that your life becomes more healthful and more safe. Other authority figures like a doctor or religious leader can also help you see that change needs to take place. I know someone who in her seventies was mugged outside of her home. When she went to her doctor to be examined, he suggested that she move to a senior community like his mother did. This person took his advice, even though she had not given any previous thought to moving.

I will now share a talk I gave to a group of adult children

on relating to our aging and possibly failing parent. I will elaborate on some of the concepts later on in the book. These ideas should be a call to action. Do not let the current tenuous situation continue. Do something.

Ah, Your Aging Parents

Ah, your aging parents! They did care for you. They do care for you. You need to care for them in a different way now. What do you do? Where do you turn? What framework can we use to understand what needs to be done?

A Biblical passage from Exodus 24:7 is often translated as "We will do first, and afterward, understand." It is a declaration of faith and trust. So I suggest that with your aging parents, you do something first, take specific actions, and then make certain that you understand your parents and their history in order to help them in making these transitions and meeting their future needs.

What usually happens with our elderly parents is that they have been aging all along, but we visit them one time and notice that they just are not what they used to be. Maybe it is a cognitive change. Maybe it is a physical change. Maybe both. Maybe this newest change is gradual; maybe it is sudden. But there will come a time when you or your siblings or other relatives will know that the current situation is not working. Maybe Mom needs to give up driving. Maybe Dad left the stove on after he was done cooking. Maybe they are not eating properly or they have left the phone off the hook one too many times. Options open to you are helping them yourself or finding aides to help them with the cleaning or cooking or driving or overseeing the taking of their medications. Do you have the time to give help like this, or is the distance to where they live a problem? I suggest you have a professional assessment done by a geriatric social worker. She can discuss the issues with you and meet with your parents to assess them directly. The solutions may be as easy as purchasing some assistive devices or remodeling their home or apartment. As people are now trying to make their houses "green," so it may be time to make your parents' home "gray" by securing or removing area rugs, simplifying the laundry process, widening the doorways to accommodate wheelchairs, installing easier-to-grasp faucet or cabinet handles, or adding lifts on staircases. Healthcare publications show a wide array of helpful devices. Additionally, perhaps their neighbors who have been lending a hand could help on a more regular basis. Or the answer may be to hire help or to have your parents move into a senior citizen building or an assisted living facility.

What if the indications are that a move to a senior building is appropriate, but your parents do not want to move? Please take them on site visits to three places. You should also put their names on the waiting lists of as many facilities as you can. You just cannot predict when a place will become available or when they will feel ready to move. If their situation is deteriorating, and you know they have to move but do not want to, a logical statement you should make to them is: "This situation has become a matter of health and safety, and I now have to make those kinds of decisions. You will have to move, but you have the choice as to whether you move to this place or that place or the third place."

To the seniors, I say please know that you should have power over your own situations as long as you are safe. But sometimes, you do not realize or want to admit that your lifestyle needs to be improved. To the children of adult parents, I say please know that these life-changing decisions, especially if they are not agreed upon by your siblings, can be difficult to make. But health and safety are the overriding considerations, and someone has to take the lead.

I have three kinds of experience in these matters. First is the situation with my mother-in-law. She came to live with us, because she realized that she was not able to be on her own any longer, and we understood that she would not take advantage of the socialization a senior residence offered. So we remodeled the garage into a mother-in-law apartment, and she lived there for nine years. During that period, she developed Alzheimer's disease. At first, we took care of her but eventually hired a helper to be with her while my husband and I were at work. Then as she became more dependent, we had to get three shifts of helpers so she would be safe around the clock. But the day came when she needed even more help than this loving team could offer her, so we moved her into a nursing home, where she stayed for several months before she died. It was the right course of action for her and for that period of our lives.

Second is the very different story of my parents. On a trip to see them, I noticed that they were not eating well and that things around the house were being neglected. I suggested that when they come to visit me the next time, we should shop around at the senior buildings in my area. They said no, that they were fine and that they did not want to move. But soon some of their friends began to move to senior buildings, and, as teenagers succumb to peer pressure, they decided that they would just "look" at senior places. They found a lovely apartment at a three-level care facility five minutes from my house, almost too good to be true, and after the definite trauma of moving and getting resettled, they actually did say that they should have moved long ago. They both gave up driving and settled down to a new pace of life. And when my father died, my mother found that she had a sisterhood of women around her, neighbors who had taken care of ailing husbands, and therefore the grieving process was softened because of their understanding.

Third is my professional experience. As the director of a high-rise senior citizen building, part of my job was to interview the applicant and the family to see if this building was the proper housing situation. There were several kinds of applicants: ones who did not meet the financial requirements, ones who were eager to make the life-style change, and ones who were being dragged there and were not going to move there to "die in a nursing home." Actually, the senior building was not a nursing home, and when I gave the tour and explained about the activities, most of the applicants saw that it might be the right place to live. Those who said, "There will be no one here like me" were often very soon making dinner dates or taking afternoon walks with new friends or playing bridge or bingo or both.

So my three tiers of experiences have taught me that you seniors may be all right on your own until matters of health and safety make it such that a change has to be made. It has also been my personal and professional experience that when people move into facilities that give more levels of help, they are grateful and most say they wished they had moved much sooner.

How do you know if it is the right change? You just have to do your homework to see all your options about home modifications and additional care or about moving. Start the planning process before you need to make the changes, so you can make the decisions less stressfully. It is certainly easier to make decisions when you are not in a crisis mode.

These are the "actions" you can take. Now for the "we will understand" component.

How much do you really know about your parents? Do

you understand where they came from, what they have done in their lives, and what their motivations are? Do you know their family histories? When they are gone, what specifics will you have of them? If you record their life stories, you will have their life memories. In my family history business called Let Us Remember, I interview seniors who often say to me before we begin: "My family already knows about my life" or "I have nothing to say" or "I cannot remember what happened to me." But as I ask them questions that are organized chronologically, psychologically, and philosophically, they engage. They start to look younger and more relaxed as their eyes twinkle at certain memories or tear up at others. In fact, I have observed that it is not unusual for men to cry when they talk about their mothers and for women to cry when they talk about their children. I often hear my clients say, "No one ever asked me that question before." Also, it is meaningful to me when the adult children tell me that they never knew certain stories that they had heard on the tapes or CDs or had read in the transcripts.

While we are talking about the history of your family, please label the back of old photographs. It is so frustrating to look at these photos and not know who is in them or where or when they were taken. Whether you hire someone to record your parents' life stories or you do it yourself or you have the grandchildren do it, the important thing is to make the time to have the interviews. To take time for the understanding.

So in relation to your aging parents, I have started this talk with an idea from Exodus and will end with a passage from Deuteronomy:

> Remember the days of old;
> Consider the generation long past.
> Ask your father, and he will tell you,
> Your elders and they will explain to you.

Food for the Sandwich Generation

Here is another concept for adult children to use when dealing with their parents and with the added responsibilities of dealing with their children. When you face this situation, you are part of what is called the sandwich generation, as you feel the tug by the generation before you and the one after you at the same time. On May 14, 1992, an article I wrote on this topic was published in the *Washington Post*. I will paraphrase "Food for the Sandwich Generation: The Meanings Behind the Bread You Choose" here. It is my hope that if you are part of the sandwich generation, these ideas will help you to think out of the box (or breadbox).

I observed that when the caller announces that she is the nurse, you might be guessing if it is the school nurse or the nurse in the cardiac care unit. I also asked if your conversations at dinner parties now centered equally around vignettes of both your youngest and oldest relatives. And I wondered if you find yourself sandwiched in the middle of caring for your children and helping your parents.

I went on to explain how you can cope with these double demands on your time and energy and how some people work out the intricacies of the life cycle web better than other people do. My suggestion was that the secret may lie in how you prepare your life's sandwich, how you choose to view the situation. Just as in a deli, when you are asked what kind of bread you would like for your sandwich, you also can make the symbolic choice of what kind of bread you want to define the way you are able to handle your responsibilities in the sandwich generation. I then listed some choices of bread and what they mean.

My first example was White Bread, like the traditional Wonder Bread. You may feel like Wonder Woman or Wonder Man as you do everything for everyone. But as with some white bread, you may wind up lacking the necessary vitamins and minerals and feeling exhausted at the prospect of doing it all yourself. I warned that the reality of the situation demands that you change the recipe of your sandwich a bit and suggested that you add a heaping tablespoon of independence on the younger generation slice of bread. You could also guide your children into helping their grandparents to deal as best they can with their age capabilities and geographic boundaries. Importantly, you should dissolve any guilt you may feel by knowing that when you let generation one and generation three cook together, they should meld into a unified family.

The next type of bread I explained was Whole Wheat

Bread, which is better for you, because the kernel is left in, and, symbolically, it allows you to maintain your kernel of existence. My guidance was that you have to decide to do things for yourself. You have to say, "I am not available now." You have to make an effort to read that book, take that vacation, or relax on that porch when you want. The demands on your time always will be there, but you will become more successful at handling everything when you are more of a person for yourself.

Then I wrote about Rye Bread, saying that you need your wry sense of humor. I suggested that you should step back from the situation and laugh. I agreed that it is sad to see your ailing parent, but I know that you can find something to laugh at. Maybe like the seeds in rye bread, your humorous episodes are few and far between, but they are there.

Something else used to make a sandwich is a Roll, so you should remember to "roll" with the punches. I reminded people that there are video cameras someone else can use at your daughter's school play so that you could be with your hospitalized dad. She will understand, because you are teaching her that life is filled with difficult choices. It is a comforting thought that when you are pulled in two directions at once you are showing compassion for your aging parent at the same time that you are serving as a "role" model for your children.

The final bread I spotlighted was Multi-Grain Bread, which some advocates say is the most healthful kind.

Since many grains go into it, it follows that this is the healthiest way for the sandwich generation to cope. My advice was for you to make use of multi-services. I asked of all the people you know, who can cook meals for your parents? Who can drive them to an appointment? Who can help you with figuring out their bills? The lesson was that you do not have to do it all. Take advantage of social service departments where professionals can give specific advice. Also, look at voluntary assistance agencies, and ask advice of a friend who has been in a sandwich before. I warned that you want to avoid the end of the children's song, "The Farmer in the Dell," since you do not want people to say of you, "The cheese stands alone." You will be mentally healthier if you allow yourself to be part of a multi-grain team.

I noted that you might feel like having a different sandwich on different days, so you should try different breads. The real question is what kind of sandwich do you want to be? I suggested that one of multi-grain and rye might become your favorite combo—keeping your sense of humor as you take advantage of help offered by agencies, family, and friends. I also pointed out that you do not have to be a Hero sandwich, which is probably too much for any one person to chew. My lesson is that if you find that you are overwhelmed or are not satisfied with how things are going, your sandwich is getting stale, and you should change your bread by taking a slice from another kind of loaf.

I concluded with the advice that you should not forget why you like sandwiches anyway, that they are cohesive units with your specific choice of bread hugging the filling, keeping it and you connected with satisfying love.

Mental Inventory of Your Living Situation

Where do both you and your parent stand? If it is on a slippery area rug, then you know you have some work to do. The first step is to take a mental inventory of how you both perceive the living situation. Choose a visit when people are not tired or upset about a recent issue. Designate a third person to write down the answers and the highlights of the discussion. Then take these tests. Give an honest answer and then discuss. Only one person may talk at a time, and each person has to be allowed to finish his thought before any other person speaks. If there is crying, everyone waits until that person feels able to speak once again. For the issues where you agree, decide how to proceed. For the issues where you disagree, reach a compromise. If it is a health or safety issue, compromise may not be possible or the compromise may not seem fair to one person or another.

Senior Housing Test
Part A—for Seniors
1. Do you feel safe where you live?
2. Do your friends and family feel you are safe where you live?

3. Do you have proper nutrition?
4. Do you take your medications on time?
5. Do you want more activities and socialization than you currently have?
6. Do you need to stop driving now?
7. Do you have a way to reach someone in case of an emergency?
8. Do you have a general power of attorney, a power of attorney for health care, and an advance directive for health care?
9. Do you wish that everyone would leave you alone?
10. Do you feel ready to re-define your independence?

Part B—for Adult Children
1. Do you feel your parent is safe in his home?
2. Do you call your parent, and she does not answer even though she is there?
3. Do you see safety issues in his home?
4. Do you feel she is not eating well?
5. Do you worry that your parent is not going to turn off the stove?
6. Do you have to repeat directions to your parent, and she still does not follow them?
7. Do you feel that you do not have the time or energy to continue to help your parent?
8. Do you feel frustrated that your parent is not what he used to be?
9. Do you see that he is not taking his medications properly?

10. Do you feel ready to help your parent re-define his independence?

There may be anger and unfinished business that comes from these tests. I am not asking you to be your own therapists. I am asking you both to hear what the other says, to see the troublesome issues from each other's point of view. Once you have expressed your own feelings and heard his or her own feelings, then you are ready to proceed. So it is now no longer a viable argument to say that you are not ready to fix what people know are problems, that is to fix your current home or to move to a senior residence. You will have made a list of what the issues are and now will be able to use the tools to fix the problems. These tools are the keys to your future living experience and to your happiness for the years ahead.

You have to make some decision. Even not deciding is making a decision to put it off. Maybe staying in your home with added services is the right decision. Maybe it is not. You and your family need to do your homework to see what is available to you.

Keys for Seniors:
- Re-define independence to make your life safer and easier.
- Your dignity is your self-respect, and no one can take that from you.

- You are the star of your life, but now your have to deal with a director.
- View your living situation from the outside for a moment.
- You can make decisions on your own, but you now may have specific limits to making those decisions.
- Apply the advice you would give to others to yourself.
- Make three site visits to senior living facilities.
- Put your name on all the appropriate waiting lists.
- You may need to hear and accept this message: "You will have to move, but you have the choice as to whether you move to this place or that place or the third place."
- Do your housing homework before the crisis.
- Record your life story.
- Label all photographs.
- Take the Senior Housing Test—Part A.
- Make a list of the issues, and fix the problems.

Keys for Adult Children:
- Do not let the current tenuous situation continue.
- Step in for matters of health and safety.
- You are now the director to his star.
- You may need the help of an authority figure like an attorney, a geriatric case manager, a doctor, a religious leader, or a favorite relative or friend to show your parent more realistic options.
- Take action, or like the director you now are, yell, "Action."
- You will do, and you will understand.

- Help your parent yourself, or find aides to help him.
- Have a professional assessment done by a geriatric social worker.
- Make your parent's home gray.
- Take your parent on site visits to three senior living facilities.
- Put your parent's name on the appropriate waiting lists.
- You may have to say this line: "This situation has become a matter of health and safety, and I now have to make those kinds of decisions."
- Do the housing homework before the crisis.
- Record your parent's life story.
- Help him label all the photographs.
- Decide what bread you are in the Sandwich Generation.
- Take the Senior Housing Test—Part B.
- Make a list of the issues, and fix the problems.

Chapter 3
Doing the Homework

"I Don't Want to Move to a Nursing Home"

Often when seniors are thinking about leaving their house or apartment, they immediately think that they will have to go to a nursing home. This statement is filled with prejudice against nursing homes. You might need to move to a nursing home, but that is something about which your doctor and the nursing home admissions staff will advise you. You probably have this thought out of fear of change or fear of dying. But it just may not be the right time for you to have that address. There are many other housing options available to help make your life safer and less worrisome to you and your family. How you succeed at senior living depends on looking at the available options and making the wisest decision based on needs, wants, and safety.

Professional Assessment

A good first step is to have an assessment done by a geriatric case manager, social worker, or an elder care specialist. These professionals should have training in or knowledge about social work, counseling, nursing, gerontology, which is the study of aging, and geriatrics, which is dealing with the care of the elderly. They should be familiar with the housing and service opportunities in your community. After they interview you and your family and see your current home, they should give you a list of options and a care plan, explaining what steps should be taken to provide for your health and safety, both now and in your future. Their unbiased evaluation should be a catalyst for discussion and next actions. They should also be able to arbitrate through your family dynamics during this emotional time.

Family Dynamics like "Goldilocks and the Three Bears"

Regarding family dynamics, yours could be like "Goldilocks and the Three Bears," where one member may be too optimistic about the situation, one may be too pessimistic, and one may even be in denial that there is any problem. Someone in the group needs to facilitate a compromise that will be just right. A helpful break to any stalemate may be to assign each relative to take on the role of another character, to walk in his shoes, to see his thought process. This technique may help you all arrive at a mutually acceptable solution. It could be that you will never get to the point where everyone is satisfied, but you have to do something for the sake of heath and safety.

Thinking About Living and Dying

When you are all thinking about these aging issues, your thoughts may fluctuate between living and dying. It is important to discuss with the family your wishes about how you want to live now and how you want to die. You adult children do not want the scenario that after your mother has died, you could only guess at her wishes. Then how would you know what necklace was important enough for her to want a granddaughter to have it or what cut glass pitcher she cherished? You might fear that if you talked to your father about his wishes relating to his end of life, he would think you want him to die. The reality is that Dad has already given the matter a great deal of thought, and if you have not discussed these difficult questions with him, you are the one left in the dark.

An AARP study in 1998 showed that 80 percent of adult children said that they have helped their parents, while only 63 percent of parents agreed. This gap in communication can be lessened with direct discussions about important age-related topics such as end-of-life attitudes. But if you do not ask, you may never know what your parents really think about these topics. Following Sir Francis Bacon's theory that knowledge is power, you now have a test which is a tool that can help you through one of the most difficult of times, the death of a parent. This "Not in the Dark Test" should help shed light on your parent's thought process for his or her end of life wishes. Divided into the categories of wishes pertaining to dying, finances, and legacy, it allows your parent to communicate to you his desires and feelings pertaining to this stage of his life. Have him take the test now, then see if his answers change in a few years.

Not in the Dark Test
(Questions 1-4 deal with death, 5-6 deal with finances, and 7-10 deal with their legacy)
1. What do you fear about death?
2. What are your wishes about a living will and power of attorney and health care directives?
3. Where do you want to be buried?
4. What would you like your funeral to include?
5. How do you want your money and assets divided?
6. What possessions do you want each person to have after you are gone?
7. What made you happy in your life?
8. What made you sad in your life?
9. How do you want to be remembered?
10. What blessings do you want to leave each family member?

After your parent takes the test is a good time to have the important talk, in which both of you communicate your feelings, fears, and annoyances and then hear the same from your loved ones. It is the time to be honest. The best technique is to leave past hurts out of this conversation. It is now the time to move ahead and certainly is the time to get your affairs in order. This test can be a valuable conversation starter, or it can be a continuation of an argument of unproductive familial patterns. How you approach the discussion and how you respond and follow through can decide its value for your family and your future relationship.

Rules for the Conversation and Active Listening
1. The oldest person talks first.
2. Only one person talks at a time.
3. There should be no yelling or cursing.
4. The conversation stops until the speaker finishes crying.
5. Someone writes down the major points of the conversation.
6. You make a plan of who does what to deal with the issues.
7. Both speaker and listener must show respect for people's feelings.

I ran a workshop in which I taught my residents the principles of Active Listening, originally formulated by Dr. Thomas Gordon. Here are some of the points from that workshop. When you use active listening, you communicate acceptance. You listen first, and then you react "actively." You do not threaten, command, preach, or lecture. You do search for the underlying, actual message. Use door openers to hear what the other person is saying: Oh. I see. Really. That is interesting. Use "you" messages to reflect the other person's ideas and feelings. You are angry because... You are worried because... Use "I" messages to communicate your thoughts and feelings. I feel frustrated... I am angry when... Do not say things like "You are stupid." Decide who owns the problem: He, I, We (the one which is adult-to-adult communication). Set limits to the communication. Choose an appropriate time and place. Assure confidentiality. Provide for a follow-up meeting. Do what you can to maintain the dignity of all persons involved. This method of active listening can be used to enhance all your relationships. It will certainly help when you have the conversations about difficult topics with your family.

Seven Topics for the Necessary Conversation Led by the Parent

1. Things I am worried about.
2. Things I am afraid about.
3. These are my health issues.
4. How I envision my funeral.
5. This is my financial situation.
6. This is my advice for you.
7. This is how I want to be remembered.

Seven Topics for the Necessary Conversation Led by the Adult Child

1. Things I am worried about regarding you.
2. Things I feel can stay the same.
3. Things I feel must change immediately.
4. Things I feel should change at a future time.
5. What I can start to do or continue to do for you.
6. What I can no longer do for you.
7. What I will remember about you.

Financial and Health Concerns

Regarding your concerns, you as the parent, with someone's assistance if needed, should make a list of your assets and liabilities and project how much money you will have to live on for the next decades. You may want to research reverse mortgages. The equity that you have put into your home possibly can now be drawn down in payments from the lender. There are age and residential requirements, and the amount that you may be able to receive is dependent on your age, interest rates, and the value of your home. The reserve mortgage is due when the borrower moves from the home, dies, or sells the home. The loan is repaid through the sale of the home. The reverse mortgage may not be the best financial arrangement for you, so you need to consult a financial expert. It is one of your options.

Another option may be long-term care insurance. Since

the costs of housing and health care can be considerable, this is one way to help to cover your expenses. As with any financial venture, you will have to weigh the plusses and minuses of such insurance, and only deal with an established company. This kind of insurance may also be used for costs related to home health, assisted living, adult day care, and other senior facilities, but depending on the terms of the policy. You should be familiar with the requirements regarding age, daily benefits, length of benefits, waiting periods during which you pay for care yourself, deductibles and copayments, inflation features, premium features, and reasons for denial of payment. As with any document, read the fine print.

In regard to your health concerns, what usually comes out of these serious conversations is that you do not want to be a burden or that you do not want to be the caregiver. Maybe you already are a burden and do not realize it. Perhaps some of this burden on your children could be lifted by your getting more help or by your moving to a place that offers various levels of support or care. When I hear people say that they do not want to be "put away in a nursing home," I sometimes think that it would make certain decisions much easier if parents would say, "When it is my time, please put me in a nursing home." Since no one has a crystal ball, we are not in a position to make promises about health-related issues. We can only do our homework to see what our options are.

Power of Attorney, Living Will, Durable Power of Attorney for Health

You should contact an elder law attorney, who can give you guidance about what documents you need for your estate planning and your medical care. You should grant a general power of attorney to your adult child, in case of emergency, and make sure it allows him to conduct your financial transactions, if you are no longer able. This elder lawyer should help you with your will and advanced directives, which include a living will, which explains the kinds of health care you do or do not want, and a durable power of attorney for health care, also called health care proxy, where you choose a person to make decisions for you in the event you are no longer able. Your desires about medical decisions, captured in these documents, are meant to convey your wishes if you are unable to speak for yourself.

The legality of these documents differs from state to state, so it is important that wherever you live, you make sure that they are valid. A Do Not Resuscitate (DNR) order can also be part of your wishes, but it is only valid if it is signed by a doctor and then put into the patient's chart. The instatement of the health privacy or HIPAA regulations, first enacted in the Administrative Simplification provisions of the Health Insurance Portability and Accountability Act of 1996 (HIPAA, Title II), required the U.S. Department of Health and Human Services (HHS) to address the security and privacy of your health data. So unless someone is designated as your health care proxy when you are unable to speak for yourself, it might be that your medical information could not be released to your family. You want to make sure you have done all you can to make it easier for your family to provide you with proper care and a smooth transition during a medical crisis.

Other services offered by elder lawyers may deal with benefits like Social Security, Medicare, Medicaid, Supplemental Security Income, and food stamps, plus consumer complaints, and nursing home resident rights. They can also help you maintain a valid will, so that after your death, your heirs will be protected, and your wishes will be followed. All these legal documents should be kept in one place. My father had a "death box" next to his desk. We all had copies of the documents, which had to be updated from time to time, especially when my parents moved to another state. You also want to be sure that a relative has the keys and signed right of access to the safe deposit box.

Get and sign a living will, a durable power of attorney for health care, and a general power of attorney. Check with your own attorney and with the laws in the state where you live or will be moving to see what is appropriate there. Some of these documents will have to be presented at the time of hospitalization. In addition, you should have printed and online copies at your home and office, and at the home of parent and siblings, of lists of current medications, all doctors' phone numbers, addresses, and specialties, family member contacts, and the patient's Social Security number, Medicare and supplemental insurance numbers, and starting dates of those policies. You never know when you will get a call that your parent has been taken to the hospital, so you want to have all that information in a file at hand, so you can have it when it is needed. Do not rely on the fact that Dad keeps it in his wallet. His wallet may not make the ambulance trip along with him.

As difficult as it may be for you or for a relative who disagrees with your parent's wishes, you should have the medical staff abide by what is written. When my mother-in-law entered a nursing home during the last horrible stages of Alzheimer's disease, we followed her wishes and had her listed as DNR—Do Not Resuscitate. As I informed one of the nursing assistants there, she asked something like why do you want to do that? So be sure to explain to all physicians and attending staff that this designation reflects the patient's own decision when he or she was well. It is important to remember at times like these that you want to follow the wishes of the patient, not the staff.

Another type of document you might want to write after the heart-to-heart talk is an ethical will. People have called this thoughtful will a love letter to your relatives. Some topics about which you may want to write, even if you have already discussed them, may be: blessings to family members, your values, your burial wishes, your life's lessons, and how you would like to be remembered.

Financial Records

You or your financial caretaker should keep careful records of your expenditures in regard to your home and medical expenses. When you are presented with a bill for charges that are unfamiliar to you or purchases you did not make or services you did not request or receive, you should question these entries. Some wordings of the entries may be necessary for your Medicare coverage or for your housing situation, but it is your right to question them and to understand them. Look at your Medicare Summary Notice and the Explanation of Benefits for charges for anything you did not receive, billing for the same thing more than once, and services not requested by your doctor. It is a good idea to keep a record of your medical appointments, why you went, what the doctor advised, and the purpose of your medication. If this is in a journal or chart form, then when someone else has to help you, it will be easier for that newcomer.

If you are a caregiver for your parent, you may be eligible to claim your parent as a dependent on your tax return. There are requirements regarding income and levels of support, so you should ask your tax preparer. Also, if you pay a certain proportion of your parent's medical care, including nursing home or assisted living costs, you may be able to take a tax deduction. Your financial planner will be able to advise you about how to use you parent's accounts to pay for health care and demonstrate how to use the taxable assets before the tax-deferred retirement accounts.

While you are questioning items, it is a good time to remember the hazards of scams. You may receive phone calls, emails, or letters from what sound or look like imposing organizations. Never give out your personal information over the phone or on a form, unless you can verify the identity of the requester. Shred documents you no longer need that include your Social Security number or credit card numbers. Do not carry your Social Security card or Medicare card in your wallet except on days you know you will need them. Scam artists are usually very good at what they do, and they are willing to prey on those who blindly follow.

Health Care and Insurance

Everyone agrees that the benefits from Medicare and Medicaid are complicated. A geriatric case manager, an admissions officer at a senior facility, or the benefits manager at the Medicare and Medicaid offices will be able to explain the rules and eligibility requirements. Because of the complex information in these areas, it is a good idea to learn about them before you are in the midst of a medical or housing crisis. Keep in mind the difference between the two. Medicare is the federal program that provides medical insurance for people over age 65. Medicare Part A automatically begins at this age and helps to pay for inpatient hospital care, limited skilled nursing care, hospice care, and some home health care. Medicare Part B is medical insurance that helps pay for the services of doctors, outpatient hospital care, and some other medical services. A monthly premium must be paid to get Part B. Medicare Supplemental Insurance is a private insurance sometimes called Medigap that pays Medicare's deductibles and co-insurances. Medicaid is a public assistance program that pays for health care service for those with low income and limited assets, which could include long-term nursing facility care, some limited home health services, and some assisted living services. Check about whether a facility you are considering accepts Medicaid payment and how it complies with federal and state regulations.

Medicare Part D is optional coverage for prescription drugs. Private supplemental drug insurance to fill in the gaps between what your insurance company will pay and what you have to pay out of pocket may also be available. In either case, you want to know if the drugs you take will be covered and what the comparative costs will be. Your Medicare office and your State Health Insurance Assistance Program (SHIP) office can help to answer your questions. Some items like hearing aids may not be covered by your insurance. Again, read the fine print, even if you need a magnifier to do so.

Adult Protective Services

For those families who know their parent needs to be in a more protective environment but that parent refuses to move or make necessary changes in his home, you can turn to the Adult Protective Services (APS) in your area. The mission of this service is "to insure the safety and well-being of elders and adults with disabilities who are in danger of being mistreated or neglected, are unable to take care of themselves or protect themselves from harm, and have no one to assist them." APS caseworkers investigate reports of abuse, neglect, and exploitation of a reported vulnerable adult, whom they define as "a person who is being mistreated or is in danger of mistreatment and who, due to age and/or disability, is unable to protect himself or herself." When they receive a call to the hotline or their office, they assess a person's risk and his ability to give informed consent. Then they make a plan and evaluate how it is being followed. Some services they can provide or arrange to be provided include emergency shelter, home repair, meals, transportation, financial management, home health services, and medical and mental health services. The person who has the capacity to understand his circumstances has the right to refuse help. You can also consult with an attorney if you need to be appointed legal guardian, conservator, or custodian for your parent. This process involves a court-ordered competency assessment and may involve taking over financial responsibility.

Other helpful agencies in your state may include the

following: Department of Aging, Family Violence Council, Long-Term Care Ombudsman, Office of the Attorney General, and Office of Health Care Quality. There is also a service called Elder Mediation. These people function like family counselors who are trained to assist you in coping with the changes that aging brings. They can help you create a plan for the future and deal with tense family dynamics, since they are unbiased third parties.

Two Daughters Talking on an Airplane to Miami

So maybe you went from being a carefree empty nester or a newlywed or someone dealing with your own health issues to being a caregiver. Now you find yourself having the "death" talk, thinking about end of life scenarios, and involving yourself in the financial situation of your parent. It may seem as though it happened overnight. On the other hand, maybe it was evolving over several years. Now you are in the midst of this depressing and consuming time of your life. It can be a significant burden to bear. You need to make divisions in your daily activities so that you do something for your parent, something for the other members of your family, and something for yourself. Listen to the conversation between Sally and Lenore, who happened to sit next to each other on an airplane bound for Miami.

Sally: Hello. Are you headed to Florida for a vacation?
Lenore: I wish. My father is not doing so well, and I have to check on him.

Sally: At least he is in a good place. Miami has so many senior care options for you.

Lenore: They do have so many that it is almost overwhelming. But that is not the problem. He insists that we will only move him out in his coffin, but the house is falling apart, and he is not bathing or taking his proper prescriptions. He is as stubborn as my teenager is. My dad refuses any help I bring in. He says they steal from him or they are the wrong color or all they do is talk on their cell phones the whole day. He drives to his early bird dinner each day, putting other commuters at risk. But because of that outing, I know that he is eating one good meal a day.

Sally: At least you have a relationship with your father. My mother and I have had a bad relationship since I dropped out of college. She makes it so unpleasant that I really do not have it in my heart to arrange for help for her. She lives in a senior building and for what she is paying is wasting her money. She does not do any of the activities and does not even go down to the dining room for dinner.

Lenore: My sister says that I am wasting our inheritance on paying for help for Dad. My brother says it is Dad's money, and we should spend it on him. I first thought we could not afford anything, but I learned about services from the area aging offices and now know that we can afford the help, if only he would accept it. Then he could stay in his house. Maybe we should have our parents trade living places. Mine needs the care, and yours does not want the services available to her.

Sally: That's funny. It is so hard to know what is right for our parents. How did they ever know what was right for us when we were growing up? And what makes it even harder is that my brother says that there is nothing wrong with Mom. When he calls her, she is pleasant and asks the right questions. But he does admit that she asks them over and over again.
Lenore: I am just doing the best that my dad will let me do.
Sally: That is a good coping mechanism. I think I will adopt that. We can only try.
Lenore: I worry about the next crisis. I have done some pre-planning, but it is so hard for me to keep taking time off from work. My boss no longer has his parents, and he really does not understand why I have to see my dad so often. Actually, my husband does not really understand all the time and money I spend checking in on my dad.
Sally: On a certain level, my mom does realize that I should not have to keep coming here to see how she is doing. But because of her depression, she is not able to function as she used to. My sister is of no help. She does not ever call Mom and says I am exaggerating when I tell her a new problem. It is causing us to bicker and argue over Mom's care and her money.
Lenore: Good luck in dealing with your mother.
Sally: Same to you with your father.

Three days later, the two women ran into each other at the airport for their return trip. Lenore had her father with her and introduced him to Sally. It turns out that he had hit a fire hydrant and wrecked the front end of the car. He agreed to give up driving and after having a heart-to-heart talk with Lenore, he decided that if he could not drive any more, he did not want to be a prisoner in his house. He was coming home with Lenore to "look" at some senior buildings, just to see if there were any pretty women there. Sally was not as successful in solving her issues, but she did meet with the social worker at her mom's building. They both decided to send in an aide to help her mother get bathed and dressed each morning. She was not going down to dinner, because she thought she smelled bad and was afraid to take a shower herself. Sally also put her mother's name on some assisted living facility waiting lists, just in case.

These two women are living through the difficult times of watching their parents age and trying to figure out how to make the process safe and comfortable for them. They both took a passive approach and suffered the related stress and upheaval of family relationships and work pressure. But they did have deep conversations with their parents, who were now ready to help identify the underlying problems causing their unhealthful behavior.

Where to Turn

So where do you turn? What is the right living situation? How do adult children know when to mix in and when to step back? Listen carefully to what is behind the issue, ask thought-provoking questions, and do your homework, so you are prepared for what is around the aging corner. Here are important options available for all of you.

Government Resources and Other Programs

Since the signing of the Older Americans Act in 1965, the Department of Health and Human Services has overseen the Administration on Aging (Public Inquiries at 202-619-0724) and Medicare and Medicaid (800-MEDICARE). The Eldercare Locator (800-677-1116) can help you find services in your area. Requests for information about aging issues and Administration on Aging programs may be sent by email to aoainfo@aoa.hhs.gov. The Resources chapter at the end of this book lists more information. Following are some of the services offered by the entities supported by Administration on Aging, with some examples from around the country:
TRANSPORTATION—These programs could make it easier for you to get to places like medical appointments, shopping and senior activities. Door-to-door transportation might be available in your area. An example in the Greater Washington, DC, area is MetroAccess, which is a shared-ride paratransit public transportation service. It provides accessible transportation curb to curb for people with disabilities who are unable to use accessible fixed route service on the bus or subway system.
VOLUNTEER ESCORT SERVICE—This service can provide someone to take you to an appointment or a visit. An example is the shopper escort service provided by

many cities, counties, or states. One in San Francisco, CA, recently received a large personal donation to form a private and public partnership to fund its new Medical and Shopping Senior Escort Service. The program in Glastonbury, CT, offers volunteers to travel with a senior or disabled person using their Dial-A-Ride or ADA Connecticut Transit minibuses. Another example is in Albany, NY, which is for shopping, medical appointments, banking, and personal errands for seniors who are independently mobile.

OUTREACH—This is an effort to inform people about services offered and to determine who could be aided from such services. They can help in referral to assistance and provide services like the one in Toms River, NJ, which has a Reassurance Telephone Line providing a daily phone call at a specified time.

MANAGEMENT HELP—Other options that can be provided by your state or local Agency on Aging are case management services, in-home services, home health workers, homemaker aid, chore service, home delivered meals, and friendly visitors.

HOME UPKEEP—For issues involving your home, there are programs of legal assistance, state insurance counseling and assistance programs, housing services like information and referral, landlord-tenant dispute resolution, tenant group support, home equity conversion, carpentry, minor electrical and plumbing repairs, low cost weatherization material, and energy assistance.

RESPITE CARE—Agencies on Aging can give information on respite care, which provides supervision for your relative while you take time off. This program gives you planned temporary substitute care. Skilled personnel can come to the home of the senior, and some nursing homes and assisted living facilities offer respite care stays there during your vacation.

PROTECTIVE SERVICES AND OMBUDSMAN PROGRAM—Adult protective services, as previously mentioned, can help when people are a danger to themselves or someone is a danger to them. There is also the Long-Term Care Ombudsman Program, which provides support to residents and caregivers in their facilities. An Ombudsman can give you information about various facilities like nursing homes and assisted living homes. For residents of those places, they deal with your problems and complaints, which are kept confidential until you grant them permission to communicate your concerns. Each state is required to have an Ombudsman Program.

One of the most valuable resources is AARP. This organization was founded in 1958, growing out of the National Retired Teachers Association (NRTA), which had been started to promote productive aging. It used to be called the American Association for Retired Persons, but now it is just called AARP. Its programs are geared for those over the age of 50, and its publications are filled with interesting ideas and services. It advocates for consumer and legal issues and provides, for example, tax preparation assistance, discounts, and the Senior Community Service Employment Program.

These government-sponsored and other programs and information outlets can give you valuable help as you decide where you should live and what services are available to you. The important steps to take are thinking about your living situation, voicing your concerns to those close to you, and then making intelligent decisions based on facts, needs, and lifestyles. See the more detailed list of resources at the end of this book.

Keys for Seniors:
- Have an assessment of your current housing situation done by a geriatric case manager, social worker, or an elder care specialist.
- Discuss with your children how you want to live and how you want to die.
- Take the "Not in the Dark Test."
- Follow the rules for this difficult conversation.
- Communicate your feelings, fears, and annoyances.
- Decide who owns each problem.
- Discuss the Seven Topics for the Necessary Conversation led by the parent.
- Sign a power of attorney, living will, a durable power of attorney for health care, and consider writing an ethical will.

- Keep careful financial records, question charges, and avoid scams.
- Learn about government resources and other programs for seniors.

Keys for Adult Children:

- Your family dynamics may be like "Goldilocks and the Three Bears."
- You do not want to guess at your parent's wishes after he has died.
- Your parent has already given his end of life issues a great deal of thought, so if you have not discussed these difficult questions with him, you are the one left in the dark.
- Listen to your parent's answers to the "Not in the Dark Test."
- Use active listening with "I" and "you" messages.
- Decide who owns each problem.
- Discuss the Seven Topics for the Necessary Conversation led by the adult child.
- Understand the topics of your parent's finances and health.
- Be prepared with legal documents, and have access to necessary information.
- Be familiar with tax and other financial requirements to help your parent.
- Learn about medical insurance before the medical crisis.
- If your parent is a danger to himself or others, know where to turn for help.
- If you become the caregiver, divide your time wisely.
- Learn about government resources and other programs.

Chapter 4
Learning About the Housing Options

"I'm Not Sure"

How do you know where you might move? The answer depends on what level of care you need and if the place is in a convenient location. It is normal to say "I'm not sure" where to apply. But when you know what each level has to offer, you should feel more comfortable in making the decisions. Here are the senior living options, explanations about them, and their good and bad points.

AGING IN PLACE

For some people, staying in your home or apartment is the right option. Others may feel that the home is too large or in need of too much repair or modification for them to remain there. Perhaps the neighbors and friends have moved away or died, so this place no longer feels right for you.

Making Your Home Safe

If you decide that you are going to stay in your home, you will want to make it safe for your aging eyes and limbs. Just because you have had that area rug for fifty years does not mean that you could not trip on it tomorrow. You and your family can take a tour of each room in your house to decide what is a potential accident waiting to happen. I have spoken to many seniors who say they do not need a cane or a walker, but they are actually unsteady on their feet. It might be best to have a third party do an assessment. A doctor or physical therapist can see if your walking or balance would be helped if you used a cane or a walker. Their proper use can relieve you of some of your anxiety of falling.

There are senior service providers who can help with an array of activities like installing assisted listening devices, organizing your closets and drawers, and arranging for transportation. There are also Certified Aging-in-Place Specialists, who are trained to suggest the modifications you need to make your environment as safe as possible. They will make a home visit and discuss what is needed to make you feel more comfortable and at less risk for injury. These changes may involve remodeling parts of your home to follow universal design principles and the accessibility standards from the Americans with Disabilities Act (ADA) of 1990. They are based on principles which should make it easier for residents whose health, mobility, vision, hearing, and dexterity have waned. Some of these features are: non-slip floors, removal of area rugs, which could cause a slip or a trip, grab bars in the bathroom, walk-in showers in place of tubs, hand-held shower heads, wider hallways and doorways to accommodate wheelchairs, floor thresholds that are even with the floor, entrance ramps, contrasting strips on the edges of steps, visual as well as audio signal smoke detectors, countertops at varying heights, chairs that lift you to a standing position, drawer handles and light switches that are easier to use, and stair lifts. I have even seen an advertisement for a large remote control, actually five inches by eleven inches, that has buttons three-quarters of an inch wide that glow in the dark. The ad said that it is almost impossible to lose. It just does not come with a live-in tutor to help you use it.

Do your children even know that you may have lost sensation in your fingers so that opening a pants or skirt hanger clasp is painful or that because of your arthritis, it is too difficult for you to button clothing anymore? Let them know so they can search for clothes with Velcro fasteners or a tool that hooks on to the buttons and so helps you pull them through the buttonholes.

Assistive Devices

An example of a helpful device is something most senior buildings have in each apartment. It is an emergency pull cord in the bedroom and the bathroom and a device for you to wear on your wrist or on a chain around your neck.

If you activate its alarm, it rings at the front desk or office. A staff person should call the apartment to ask if you are all right. If you activated it in error, he should tell you how to reset it or send to your apartment an aide who will reset it. If you do not answer, he should call an ambulance. You can have a similar personal emergency response system installed in your own home. These systems have a help button that sends a signal to your telephone even if your phone is off the hook. Then a response center monitors the call and sends help if that is what is needed. Some hospitals offer rental of this equipment. You should also have on your refrigerator a list of your medications and your emergency contacts. Most emergency medical technicians are trained to look for this information on the front of the refrigerator.

Other medical devices and aids that you may need can be prescribed by your doctor, who can fill out a Certificate of Medical Necessity. It is a document that says you require medical equipment like a wheelchair or a walker. The supplier should be able to help you determine if the cost of the equipment is covered by your health insurance.

There are electronic devices that can alert your doctor and family members if you have not moved or have not taken your medications. These home monitoring systems that you can have installed in your house or apartment remind you to do a certain task. They can also send an alarm to a centralized location if you are inactive or have not done things like opened the refrigerator or turned on the lights. A machine called the Electronic Medication Management Assistant (EMMA) automatically distributes your medication dosage. If you don't take the pills out of the machine, it transmits a wireless message to your contacts. You can also take periodic cognitive tests on the computer to track your mental alertness. Whether you view these devices as a kind of intrusive Big Brother watching over you or a relief that someone can monitor you, they will make your house or apartment "smarter" and possibly enable you to remain there safely for a longer time.

Driving or Not

Driving is another issue of family discussion, either to your face or behind your back. You would not tolerate poor driving when you are a passenger, so you should understand when a passenger in your car says that your skills are not up to par. As our eyesight and reaction time deteriorate when we age, so does our driving. I knew someone whose license was reissued to him by mail every five years. He drove well into his nineties, or rather I should say that he drove poorly into his nineties.

To sharpen your driving skills and to learn how to compensate for your age-related issues, you can take a refresher driving course, like one sponsored by AARP. Upon completion of the course, you may be able to receive an auto insurance premium reduction or discount, depending on your insurer's rules or the insurance laws in your state. You may also come to the conclusion that it is time for you to give up driving. This change means that your world does become more limited, so that may be an argument in favor of moving to an independent living place where activities and socialization are brought to you.

Proper Nutrition

Are you eating properly? Do you have a variety of foods? Are you able to shop for yourself? These are important questions when you realize that your brain needs appropriate nourishment to keep you functioning. If you are no longer able to cook for yourself and if you are eligible, you may want to have Meals on Wheels delivered to your home. After you qualify for the program based on your verifiable need and financial situation, your local agency, depending on the length of their list and their volunteers, may be able to deliver meals to your home. If you are over-income, you can look into companies that pre-package meals and deliver them to your home or apartment. There are also grocery delivery companies, that will bring what you need to your door for a fee.

Home Care

An additional option for those who want to age in place, but who need health care and other supportive services, is home care. The services provided by home care can range from something as simple as help with household chores to skilled nursing care. Home health care is paid for from your private funds, unless the care is specified by your doctor and provided by a Medicare-certified agency or is covered by your long-term care insurance. Medicaid may subsidize some of the home care services. Check your state laws and with local health departments and offices on aging regarding coverage. Some of your needs may be met by companion care, which is when someone helps you with food preparation, housekeeping, and transportation. If you are no longer able to perform the activities of daily living (ADLs), meaning eating, bathing, dressing, toileting, walking, and managing medications, then you may need the help of a home health care worker. The higher levels of care may be provided by a licensed practical nurse or a registered nurse through a skilled nursing care agency. You should only be paying for the level of care you really need.

So the steps are to determine the kind of help you need, then to interview the caregivers, and then to check references. The point is to feel safe in your own home, as you receive help to enable you to function as well as possible.

To keep your mind active and to get you out of the house to socialize, you can participate in community programs. One excellent free one for those over 50 is the OASIS, which offers a range of classes like art, wellness, fitness, computer literacy, and travel. They usually meet at shopping centers and currently serve twenty-six cities.

Managing Care from a Distance

For those adult children who live far from your parent, maybe you have chosen the option of managing your parent's care long distance yourself. This system might work for a few months, but if you add up your costs of travel, telephone bills, medical supplies, meal preparation, and home maintenance, you might be better off hiring a geriatric case manager who works near your parent. She can schedule an assessment and make a plan for proper care. Then she oversees what needs to be done.

Being a Caregiver

If you are the caregiver, you have taken on a loving and difficult job. The important things to remember are to set limits on what you are willing to do and to take time for yourself. There are other family members who can help in alternative ways, like paying for respite care or arranging for volunteers to give added help. If you do not tend to yourself by taking breaks, seeing your friends, or venting to a support group, you will diminish yourself and your capacity to provide emotional support and physical care to your relative. You have to guard against burnout, which may include symptoms of depression, anxiety, irritability, anger, exhaustion, self-criticism, withdrawal, substance abuse, trouble on your job or with your family, and eventually spiraling into hatred of your responsibilities. This list is long and serious. Before caregiving gets to be too much, take some time off. Whether the substitute help comes from a respite program or a friend, relative, or hired aide, you need to have this time for yourself or for your other obligations and interests.

Guilt and Siblings

You will feel guilty when you are away, because you are a responsible person. You probably feel guilty when you are doing the daily caregiving anyway. You have to file this guilt in the back of your mind, telling yourself that you are doing the best you can or, as I wrote earlier, the best your parent will allow you to do. If you are a sibling who is not giving care on a day-to-day basis, please think before you criticize. You have a right to express your opinion, but it is how you say it that can be the deal breaker. You should start your comments with how much you appreciate what your sibling is doing for your parent. Then using sentences that have "I" as the first word, you can explain your concerns and offer compromises and specific help you are able to do or you are able to provide.

Your aging in place may last for many years, but there also may come a day when you can no longer stay in your home. It may be because you are deteriorating or the house or apartment is. Whatever the reason, you and your family need to plan ahead for any next level of care. There is too much stress during a crisis and probably not enough time to be able to do a thoughtful and thorough job researching which is the appropriate next place to live.

The good points of this kind of housing: This housing option is possibly the one with the lowest cost. It is also the one with the least adjustment needed. Staying in one's own home means that it feels like home. It is a place that holds your memories, and that level of comfort is important. I have seen people living very well in their own homes for the remainder of their lives.

The bad points of this kind of housing: I have also been in homes of the elderly where the faucets are dripping, the placement of furniture and area rugs poses safety hazards, there are feces and urine on the toilet and surrounding floor, there are pills on the carpet where they have not realized they have dropped them or cannot bend down to retrieve them, furniture covered with dust, door locks not working properly, telephones left off the hook or not recharged, spoiled food in the refrigerator, roaches around, and garbage not taken out in a timely manner. And these residents think that they are managing well. They could be doing so much better and could be living healthier lives, if they had someone come in to make repairs, clean, exterminate, and manage their medications. In other words, they need more help, and it is up to the relatives and friends to put those services in place if the senior cannot or does not see or feel that anything is wrong. The other bad issues in this environment could be isolation and poor nutrition, which can lead to mental and physical decline.

MOVING IN WITH FAMILY

For some of you, the option of moving in with family sounds right. For others, it sounds like someone's worst nightmare. You both may be right. It just depends on your living environment, your use of time, and your relationship with each other. Both sides will need to set rules for the house and for maintaining each other's space. Some seniors are interested in helping with the childcare, and some are not interested or are no longer capable. Some may want to help with the cooking or dishwashing, while some may not.

When my mother-in-law moved in with us, we decided to have a weekly meeting with her to assess our evolving situation. During the meeting, we would define any problems and aim for solutions. We would try to end each session with an upbeat feeling. Unfortunately, as her Alzheimer's condition deteriorated, we had to tighten her circle for her safety. It was as though the layers of her personality were being peeled off like the layers of an onion by this vicious disease. She remained curious about life, but her confusion was evident in some of her questions like "Is this last night yet?" and "Who took away the wind?" We had to hire aides to stay with her while we were at work, and then eventually around the clock. We hoped to have her stay with us as long as we could provide for her a proper level of care. But when the day came that we had to move her to a nursing home, she was at a mental state where she was happy to have the attention and the stimulation of so many others around her. Her first comment was, "This is a nice place. I will enjoy it here." She only had three months there, and we were grateful for the care she received.

The effect on our family during the nine years she lived with us was interesting. The children, who were young at the time, did not quite understand what their grandmother was going through, but they saw how she needed our help and emotional support. We know we set an example for care for a relative. We took it one problem at a time and had backup plans for when her dedicated aides could not come.

Dealing with Giving Care

How does one even know what to do as a caregiver? You know the basic physical routines that your parent may need. And you probably have been supplying the emotional care for the last few years. Some people call this role reversal, when a parent becomes like a child and the adult child becomes like a parent. But others say that you can never take the place of your parent. You will make your own semantic choice. The point is that someone for whom you feel responsible needs more help. How you and your family deal with this new stage is something you all have to work out. It may happen overnight when your father is released from the hospital or the rehab unit at a nursing home after his stroke, or you may have observed the evolution of your mother's mental deterioration so you know that in a month she will be moving in with you. To help you learn about caregiving, there are classes through organizations like the Red Cross Caregivers Program. Local hospitals and nursing homes may also offer classes in home care. Some families hire a home health aide for a week and learn care techniques from her.

The impact of any type of caregiving on you and your family will depend on your relationship with your parent, with the other members of your nuclear family, and with your siblings. There is no denying the potentially debilitating toll that caring for a deteriorating parent can take on you and your family. You may become mired in feelings of anger and resentment and mourn your lack of control and privacy. The irony is that your own health can suffer while you are caring for the health of your parent. You need to organize your days so that you can do the caregiving chores, meet the needs of your spouse, children, grandchildren, friends, and job, and give yourself some breathing time. You need to be honest in realizing the things you cannot or will not do. This point is when you should work out a responsibility routine with siblings, friends, or hired aides. If you cannot afford to pay people, you can work out a barter relationship where you will do something for that person and she will help to do something in your busy home. It may be that you do not feel comfortable bathing your parent or you do not have strength to cook dinner. Find a person who can do these things for you as you exchange specific jobs in their home.

Keeping Other Family Members Informed

If you have siblings and whether they live near or far, it will still never be a fair division of duties. Some siblings contribute money instead of time. Some do absolutely nothing for their parent. For whatever reason, right or wrong, that people will not or cannot help, it is up to the caregiver to keep the other family members informed of physical, mental, and emotional changes, both in the parent and in the caregiver. Have weekly updates, and be specific in what you need from them. If you do not know or are not sure what you need, then tell them the two things that were the hardest this week. Maybe they can think of a solution. Remember to have time off through respite care for your parent or through sharing tasks with others.

For siblings who are far away physically or emotionally, the advice is the same as it was to a non-caregiving sibling who lives nearby. To review, you have to think before you criticize what the caretaker is doing or how much money he is spending. Your concerns may be legitimate, but it is also important how you approach the subject. Try to work out a compromise solution. I often hear of siblings coming to visit and then saying that there is nothing wrong with their mother or that she is not in as bad shape as you described. Remember that with conditions like Alzheimer's, the person may still retain her social graces and appear well to visitors. Trust the observations of your sibling who is onsite 24/7. Remind the caretaker how grateful you are.

Praise is important to hear. Think of ways you can make your parent and sibling feel better. Sending a bouquet of flowers once a week does not come close to making the score equal in the caregiving, but it can brighten up the room and remind people that you are thinking of them.

Hiring a Senior Aide

The hiring of a senior aide can be a blessing. You can find them through certified agencies, ads, and word of mouth. Usually, these people are gifted in patience and provide the necessary physical and emotional support for you or your parent. But your parent may totally reject any help or show constant hostility toward the aides. You need to emphasize that he is at the point where he must have help. That part is non-negotiable. But as to who is hired, he can have a say between two or three applicants. That point is where his independence can assert itself. You should listen to his complaints carefully. Is the aide really stealing or watching television or talking on her cell phone all day, ignoring him? Or does she have the television on in the background while she is doing her responsibilities?

The good points of this kind of housing: You do not have to worry from afar how your loved one is doing, because you can see her all the time. You also do not have to travel to where she is. This type of situation saves you time and energy. You may save significant sums compared to higher levels of care. You may also feel that you owe your parent this support, since she raised you.

The bad points of this kind of housing: You have a disruption to your lifestyle, a lack of privacy, and you may have to be on duty around the clock. Your personal involvement is typically higher than in other settings. You have to set limits, share the work load with other family members or professionals, and give yourself necessary down time or time off.

ADULT DAY CARE

Another alternative for those who are living independently or with family, but who need supervision during the day, is adult day care. If you are a caregiver, then the adult day care centers afford you the opportunity to go to work or to have a break during the day.

The centers can provide a social model and a medical model. The social type is usually sponsored by a community organization and provides programming to meet the needs of physically or mentally impaired adults. These day care centers offer help in the activities of daily living, which listed again are eating, bathing, dressing, toileting, walking, and managing medications. The centers also provide socialization and an array of programs, including exercise. The medical model adds health services to the social model. Many centers offer physical and occupational therapy. Adult day care centers are open during the day, but provide less than 24-hour care. Some programs offer services after business hours or on weekends and holidays. The costs are generally less than full-time staff or nursing services, and some long-term care insurance policies or state Medicaid waiver programs cover parts of the fees. If you are not able to drive your parent to the center, there may be transportation available.

The senior and caregiver both should visit several centers to see which one offers the best services and the most stimulation. You should ask to see their accreditation certificates. For example, one of the accreditation organizations, the Commission on Accreditation for Rehabilitative Facilities (CARF), maintains strict standards for adult day care facilities. You should ask about how individualized care plans are written and followed. You should observe the layout of the facility, noting where the dining room area is, how sturdy the furniture is, and if there is a place for sick participants to spend the day.

The good points of this setting: This service provides a safe place for you to be the whole day and allows your caregiver to have time off. It is a moderate cost option for care during the day. The staff should provide programming for a full array of activities for your mental and physical stimulation. You will be around other people and therefore not be so isolated.

The bad points of this setting: When you enter the facility, you might see people just sitting around unengaged or speaking inappropriately. These people should be well supervised, and at least they are in a safe environment. They have gotten out of their homes for some stimulation, which occurs not only during the course of the activities there, but also during the trip back and forth. You may not enjoy the activities or may not want to participate in them.

CONGREGATE HOUSING

Another living option is congregate housing. This program, which can take many forms, provides supportive services to seniors in independent living buildings that serve people of low-to-moderate incomes. There are specific age and income requirements to become part of this program and specific procedures for assessing residents' needs and providing services. The costs to residents are usually 30 percent of income for rent and 20 percent for services.

Congregant housing was originally a program that was like an assisted living environment in senior apartments. There was a shared meal. But it has grown to exist in apartments designated as congregate housing. These apartments, which may be freestanding or parts of a larger facility, may be fully equipped apartments or single rooms. The basic funding for congregate housing comes from the U.S. Department of Housing and Urban Development (HUD), in coordination with the Rural Housing Service of the U.S. Department of Agriculture. The program offers grants to states, local government, not-for-profit housing sponsors, and charitable organizations. Those entities use the funds to provide meals, housekeeping, and some personal assistance to the frail elderly and residents with disabilities in federally subsidized housing. It is a program based in the housing facility rather than one that moves with the resident.

Other names for congregate housing can be supported housing, life-care homes, sheltered housing, and single room occupancy housing. Board and Care homes can be subsidized for low-income seniors, but they can also have a private pay option.

Congregate housing appeals to seniors who are no longer able to live on their own, but who still would like to live in a private senior apartment where meals are prepared and housework provided. The apartment or complex should have full-time staff and recreational and social activities for the congregate residents. Some places provide transportation to appointments and help with taking medications.

The good points of this kind of housing: This type of situation is one in which people's needs are met. You are supervised by full-time staff. You have increased independence compared to some other options.

The bad points of this kind of housing: When the staff cannot come to work, someone has to fill in. Tensions may develop if you do not get along with the other residents in this home or apartment.

GROUP HOME OR COMPOUND

Another option is a senior citizen group home. There is a different category of group home that is for those who are mentally or physically disabled. A group home for seniors is usually a house with a bedroom for each resident, a common room, a dining area, and a kitchen. It is typically staffed around the clock, and the residents are supported in their activities of daily living, unless it is a group home where you must be self-sufficient.

Many group homes are privately owned, and they can be either not-for-profit or for-profit. Some are sponsored by local departments of aging and, therefore, may be subsidized. Some may be run by a live-in family and may be called a bed and care home. All group homes should be licensed by the state, so make sure you check that the home meets all those requirements. You want to ask about the reliability of the staff and what back-up plans they have. You also want to make sure the house itself appears safe. Further, you want to know what changes in your own condition would cause you to have to move out.

There are two other shared living environments in this category. One is the self-care group homes where there is no staff support since the seniors are responsible for their own care. The other is the shared compounds, where people move in to live near relatives or selected friends. Each compound sets its own rules about the responsibilities of all involved. Some groups of friends or relatives may purchase land and build a set of homes, buy several neighboring homes that are already built, or add on to or remodel areas of the family home. The compound could also resemble a campground with separate living areas and a common dining hall, so that the group of family members or friends can be separate yet together.

The good points of this kind of housing: In a group home, you are not living alone, and you do have your needs met. Depending on the type of group living situation it is, the staff members or you personally are responsible for what happens. If you have this self-direction, you feel a sense of control. The comfort level with this sense of community can be valuable. In a group compound, you probably have been able to choose the group members with whom you are living.

The bad points of this kind of housing: Since it is group living, you have to rely on others. Trouble may arise if the participants do not get along with others. You need to have plans for when residents require higher levels of care. You also need to know who makes the decision and who enforces it when one can no longer remain.

NATURALLY OCCURRING RETIREMENT COMMUNITY (NORC)

So if the time comes that you decide you want to move to a senior building, you may already be in one. If you and your neighbors have lived in the building for many years, it could be that the apartment house has become a naturally occurring retirement community (NORC).

A NORC may be a certain apartment building or a street or streets of single-family homes, where the residents have stayed for many years, so that the neighborhood became a community of senior citizens. You can seek appropriate governmental or other services to give you assistance to remain in your current home or apartment. Some examples are social activities, group excursions to concerts and museums, exercise programs, meal assistance, home and garden upkeep, and regular transportation.

If you feel that more should be done for seniors in your NORC, you can form a committee to seek additional services, apply for grants, or contact your local area on aging agency. Since people of other ages probably live in the apartment building or the neighborhood, there is the added benefit of daily intergenerational contact.

The good points of this kind of housing: You remain in your apartment or home and the community that is familiar to you. There are governmental and private grants that can supply staff to your building to set up various programs and activities.

The bad points of this kind of housing: Things have gotten old around you, as have your neighbors. If the building has not been renovated recently, the fixtures and internal structure may be showing their age. Someone or some agency has to take on the responsibility of overseeing the grant or other funding to provide staff to run the programs.

CONTINUING CARE RETIREMENT COMMUNITY (CCRC)

A continuing care retirement community, also called a life care community, is one where both your current requirements and your future medical needs are met. Its contract provides for lifelong housing of independent living, assisted living, medical care services, and long-term care including skilled nursing services.

An inviting aspect of this kind of housing is that you can move in while you are able to live independently and still remain at the facility when you get sick or become unable to care for yourself. Many of these facilities emphasize preventative health care. The services include meals, housekeeping, transportation, personal care assistance, and activities. Most CCRCs have restrictions on age, assets, income, health, and mobility. You may or may not have to move to different sections in the same facility depending on the level of care you need.

There are two parts to your financial obligation. You are responsible for an entrance fee, that in many contracts becomes part of your estate when you die, and for the monthly payments, whether you own or rent the unit. There are several types of contracts: extensive (provides unlimited long-term care without much increase in the monthly fees), modified (designates a specific amount of care beyond which you pay additional fees), or fee-for-service (requires you to pay for health services at daily nursing care rates), so you need to read all the fine print or contact an attorney to advise you on specifics for that facility.

Some CCRCs are sponsored by religious or specialty groups. For example, the Department of Veterans Affairs and a private developer have plans to construct one in the Baltimore suburbs. Others may be on the campuses of universities. There is a national Continuing Care Accreditation Commission (CCAC), which sets standards and conducts evaluations of facilities. Ask to see the evaluation of the CCRC when you visit it. Be sure to tour all the areas that provide the different levels of care to help you decide if this kind of senior housing is right for you.

The good points of this kind of housing: You are cared for in the same facility from when you move in until you die. This continuity relieves the anxiety about having to move to another setting.

The bad points of this kind of housing: You may have to pay a large entrance fee. Your neighbors are at various points along the health spectrum. When you move in as a healthy person, you may not want to be around those who are ailing. However, when you become ill, it is still your home.

INDEPENDENT LIVING

Independent living communities come in various sizes. They may be a single-family development, a high-rise or low-rise apartment building, an age-restricted community, or a condominium or cooperative. In some places, you buy the house or apartment. In some, you lease the unit. They are geared to the senior who wants an active life but needs support services and security. There usually is a full range of activities, social events, and cultural trips. There probably is a meal plan, which affords you the luxury of not cooking at all or only as much as you desire.

These communities usually have their own age or income requirements. Some may be subsidized by the U.S. Department of Housing and Urban Development (HUD) under plans like the Section 8 program, where the building may offer reduced rents or may accept applicants who have their own Section 8 voucher. The Section 8 subsidy pays for the difference between what the low-income senior can afford for rent, which is usually 30 percent of his income, and the contract rent set by HUD. This subsidy program was started to give federal housing assistance for construction or rehabilitation of low-income housing or to subsidize current housing. Another of HUD's programs is the Section 202 designation. It supplies affordable rental housing for seniors. The rent subsidies are based on adjusted gross income, found by subtracting approved medical expenses from one's gross income. Another HUD program is the Section 236 one, often found in older buildings. For this subsidy, seniors pay, depending on their income, either market rent based on a market rate mortgage or they pay basic rent, based on a percentage of their income with rent amounts never exceeding the market rents. Be sure to inquire about the rent schedules, the income requirements, how often the rent increases, and what service you get for that rent.

Some independent living communities have established relationships with nearby community centers, universities, or medical facilities, which make access to those places easy and stimulating. Communities like Leisure World appeal to the younger senior, because they have a minimum age requirement of 55 and do not have a mandatory meal program. When you are gathering information, you should ask what the average age of the residents is. If it is 85, and you are twenty years younger, you have to see if it is really the place where you want to live. A number of senior communities will allow you to use a furnished unit as a vacation rental to try out the lifestyle.

The best idea, as with buildings that provide other levels of care, is to visit them, put your name on their waiting lists, and make plans of what to do when you are offered an apartment.

The good points of this kind of housing: You have your own apartment and come and go as you please. Privacy and security are valuable assets. Your socialization and nutritional needs are usually met. You can participate in the full calendar of events.

The bad points of this kind of housing: You have to downsize and live with people who are deteriorating, who cannot hear well, and who move away or die.

ASSISTED LIVING

Assisted living places, which may also be called residential care, adult care homes, sheltered care homes, or domiciliary care, were developed to give support to seniors who could no longer live on their own, but who did not yet need a nursing home. Assisted living residents are provided with personalized levels of daily care, including some minor health care but not the skilled comprehensive support that a nursing home supplies. These places are staffed around the clock and provide help with your activities of daily living, that is, eating, bathing, dressing, toileting, walking, and managing medications. They should also supply exercise time and social and recreational activities. The scope of services may differ depending on the size and staff. Some assisted living facilities may include residents who are incontinent or who have Alzheimer's disease or other types of dementia. Some may not admit people with those diagnoses. The staff members in many of these residences use personalized care plans geared to the individuals.

Assisted living facilities are accredited by the state. You should ask to see their accreditation certificates. They may also have accreditations done by other trade organizations, but that is voluntary on their part. The regulations under which they function may differ from state to state, and services allowed in assisted living facilities in one state may only be allowed in nursing homes in other states. Some states are implementing ways to make the assisted living concept more affordable. In Illinois, there are Supportive Living Facilities (SLFs) that are assisted living places for Medicaid-eligible residents. They contribute all of their Social Security, except a monthly personal allowance, to receive housing and services.

This kind of housing provides you security in an understanding environment. You might feel relief that you now have reminders for your daily routine.

The good points of this kind of housing: Your medications are administered to you, and you are given help with bathing and dressing. Meals are provided. This level of service should help you feel safe and cared for.

The bad points of this kind of housing: There may be residents whose mental or emotional states are depressing to you. Also, there may be odors that hit you upon entering or that linger throughout the building.

NURSING HOME

If your condition has changed so that you are too sick or frail to live elsewhere, then a nursing home may be the right place. Here the care is under the direction of a doctor. You will be given physical and occupational therapies to keep you feeling as well as possible. There are varying levels of care in a nursing home, which can include short-term care, sub-acute care, respite care, and rehabilitation services. If you find yourself in a hospital, their discharge planner should help you to determine where to go after your hospitalization. It may be a sub-acute area of a nursing home and then you might have to move to their long-term care unit. You will also learn about the Medicare requirements for payment for care in a nursing home and how the diagnostic related groups (DRGs) determine the reimbursement rate to the health care facility.

It is important to visit several nursing homes in your area to see how they differ and how they are the same. Assuming all factors are equal, it is best to choose the one that is closest to the adult child's home. In each nursing home, ask if it is certified by the Joint Commission, which used to be called the Joint Commission on Accreditation of Healthcare Organizations (JCAHO), and if it is ranked by the state. If it is certified by the Joint Commission, that means it has met rigorous standards regarding patient care through on-site visits at least every three years. Ask to see a copy of the most recent state survey to view any citations for deficiencies. A nursing home must also have a state certification that meets with approval from the Centers for Medicare and Medicaid (CMS). Ask to see the home's certification of compliance, which means that it meets federal requirements. You also want to inquire about the staff-to-resident ratios and staff turnover rates. The federal Medicare program has a website at www.medicare.gov/nhcompare, that locates nursing homes, rates them on numerous criteria, and allows you to compare the ratings of several nursing homes on the same screen.

The admissions representative should give you a tour and explain the facility's philosophy. The residents should be well-groomed and appropriately dressed. It is important to see that rooms are individualized with family photos, paintings, and mementos. The atmosphere should be welcoming to the resident, the family, and other guests. Many nursing homes now have pets and plants throughout, a concept started with what was first called the Eden Alternative. They have moved away from the hospital or institutional model, so they are less impersonal. Well-run nursing homes are filled with family members who feel that their voices are heard and with residents who feel more in control of their own day. Some nursing homes are being built as a compound of small homes or cottages centered around common dining areas.

All nursing homes should have an Ombudsman, who can act as a third party to help with your complaints and concerns. This move may be your most difficult, because you are frail or sick, but it is a move meant to provide you with care and safety. The nursing home has to provide for your basic needs and then your individual concerns. There should be a wide array of activities to stimulate you and to provide socialization. The whole staff should be concerned about improving your quality of life and helping you not to be bored or isolated. People who work in nursing homes know the value this environment has on the patients. It is important to keep open the channels of communication, to make sure needs are being met and expectations are being addressed. You may feel the need to hire your own private duty nurse or aide to be at bedside during certain shifts throughout the nursing home day.

The good points of this kind of housing: You will receive needed medical care and physical therapy. Your condition will be monitored around the clock. If your diagnosis indicates that you can recover fully or at least get back some strength, you will be helped by professionals through your recuperation.

The bad points of this kind of housing: The sights, sounds, and smells may be hard to take. Patients may be moaning or screaming out for help, whether or not they really need it. It is also difficult to see loved ones visit as they remember the vibrancy their relatives once had.

HOSPICE

Hospice is a kind of care and does not have to be a specific place. The word comes from the Latin, meaning guesthouse, and was originally a place of shelter for tired and sick travelers returning from religious pilgrimages.

It is now a concept of care where teams of medical and other service personnel, volunteers, and family members deliver compassionate services like pain management and emotional and religious support to the terminally ill and their families. This care does not prolong or shorten life. The workers are trained to provide palliative care, also called comfort care, and grief and bereavement counseling. Hospice patients can receive this care in their home or someone else's home, a nursing home, a hospital unit, or a hospice center.

When you are inquiring about hospice care, you should ask about the responsibilities of the family members and how the hospice staff or volunteers can help out when you as the caregiver have to go to work or have to travel. You also want to know how the preliminary evaluation is conducted and if the company is accredited by the Joint Commission, is licensed, and is certified by Medicare or the state.

The good points of this kind of setting: They make a difficult time easier. They endeavor to teach you how to say goodbye. They also provide counseling to you after the patient has died.

The bad points of this kind of setting: Death is still death, and not every one handles it the way you would like. When my father died in a hospice facility, the nurse called to tell me, adding that I should have a nice day.

I have started this listing with staying in one's own home and ended with a deathwatch with hospice workers. These are the current options for senior housing, for living out the last parts of life. This sometimes overwhelming decision should be made only after you know all the facts and all the ramifications of making such a change. However, what you do to add to these last stages is up to you and to the environment in which you live.

Keys for Seniors:

- Know what each level of housing offers and costs.
- Tour the facilities, and view their certifications.
- Be realistic when it is time to give up driving.
- Think rationally about your current living situation.
- Voice your concerns about staying or moving to those close to you.
- Make intelligent decisions based on facts, needs, and lifestyles.
- Plan ahead for the next level of care.

Keys for Adult Children:

- Know what each level of housing offers and costs.
- Tour the facilities, and view their certifications.
- If you are geographically distant from your parent, hire a local geriatric case manager to oversee his care.
- File guilt in the back of your mind.
- If you are a sibling not giving daily care to your parent, offer whatever help you can, and think before you criticize.
- Plan ahead for the next level of care.
- Keep other family members informed.
- If you are a caregiver, ask for help, barter with friends, guard against burnout, and seek respite care.

Chapter 5
Having the Interview

"I Don't Know"

So by now you should have had the talk about where you currently live and if it is working, both silently as an internal monologue and aloud with your family. From that discussion, you should have decided what the next steps for you are. If it is staying in your home with physical modifications and additional help, then you should make a plan and follow it. If you decided that you need to move to another place, you should have researched the kinds of housing for which you qualify. Most entrance requirements are based on your level of need and your age, income, and assets. You should put your name on the waiting lists for the places that may be right for you. Then you will be called for an interview.

How do you prepare? What should you ask? What answers should you give? What should and should not happen at an interview?

During my time as coordinator of resident services and

as director of Filbert Gardens, I conducted 694 interviews. Even though I went over the same materials and gave the same tour, each one of those interviews was different. At this particular independent living facility, about a third of the people who called to get on the initial waiting list were no longer interested when asked to come in for the interview. Then about a third were not eligible or not interested in the building. Finally, about a third moved in. Of those, about three-quarters wished they had moved in years before, and a quarter probably did not like living there.

Ways Interviews Should Be Conducted

The following explains how I conducted interviews and what you can expect to happen during yours. These same principles can be used or modified during your interview for any level of senior housing for which you are applying. If you are interviewing at a place where you will need specialized levels of medical care, you want to ask very specific questions to see if your particular needs will be met there. Usually, when someone has to enter a nursing home, the adult children are the ones who meet with the admissions staff. If the applicant cannot be at the interview or take the tour of the various facilities because he is still hospitalized, then the relative should let him know what he learned at the interview and visit.

During the interviews, you want to be looking for a place where the staff treats all the family members with respect and interest. I would always shake hands with elder first, since that person was the star of the day. He was the one who might move in, and I wanted to start out our relationship on the right foot, or hand in this case. One daughter told me later that she was taken aback when I walked past her and went directly to her father to shake his hand. However, by the end of the interview, she told me she realized that she was not the center of attention here and thanked me for making her father feel important.

    I then would take the applicant by himself to my office and start out by answering his questions. I would find out where he was currently living and why he wanted to move. I often heard the answer, "I do not want to move. My son wants me to move here." I would ask why he thought the son had that desire and interesting things would come out. Many said things like his child is lazy because does not want to go down to Florida to help him when he is not feeling well, or that the new daughter-in-law will not let him move in with them. The psychological levels are intriguing, but I would say that I would make my presentation, and then they would have to work out their decision. I would use certain questions to be a barometer of one's coping skills. If I asked what is the name of his bank, and the applicant said, "I don't know," that would not concern me, because banks were changing names quite often. During one stretch of time, I was not even sure of the current name of my bank. Also, when I asked what the phone number was for their daughter and they did not know, that did not send up a red flag, because many had their phones programmed so that all they had to do was press Memory 2 to reach her. But it was a flag for me if they could not tell me their own address and phone number or how many grandchildren they had.

I would then explain what our mission was, what our particular HUD regulations were for age and income, and then invite the family to join us. If I knew at that point that this person was a good candidate for admission, I would tell the family when they entered my office that Mom was a great fit. If I knew that the person did not meet the admission requirements or was adamant about not moving in, I would explain those reasons. I would go through the activity calendar with all of them, and I would point out, based on the person's interests, what might make him happy at Filbert Gardens or at the neighboring community center. Whenever I interviewed a husband and wife at the same time, I would address one question to one person and then the next to the other person. In cases where one spouse was always more dominant or was now covering for the lack of mental ability of the other one, I would explain that it was important for me to assess each one's interest in moving and in meeting the building requirements. I would then ask for the necessary financial records and make a list for both of us of the ones they still needed to supply. If I felt that they needed a higher level of care or were not eligible to live in this building, I would give them a list of more appropriate places in our geographical area.

If I came to the conclusion that we should continue the application process, I read aloud a document to them, just so there would be no misunderstanding. It said what we had done that day, that they were now on a preliminary waiting list, what they had to supply to get on to the ready waiting list, the estimated, I repeated, estimated waiting time until an apartment might be offered, and what the time frame for moving in might be after they accepted an apartment. It is not easy to absorb all of that information, so I felt better reading it aloud in front of everyone and then giving each one a copy to take home and reread through the waiting process.

I then took the whole group on a tour of an apartment and the common areas. I always showed an apartment halfway down the long corridors to assess their mobility and strength. The woman who allowed us to show her apartment had furnishings that demonstrated how much could actually fit in the square footage. Some places show you a vacant unit, but it may be harder to visualize how much furniture you can bring there. I preferred to show the same layout of a unit for which they qualified, but one that was already furnished. However, this comfort measure does not please everyone. One daughter and her mother came complaining into my office asking what we were hiding by not showing them the unit they were to be offered. The fact that people had just moved out and it still needed to be painted and have the rug cleaned made us feel that showing their actual unit was not a better idea.

I made sure to introduce the applicant by name to all residents and staff who passed by us on the tour. I enjoyed telling each one of shared hometowns or interests. At the end of the tour, I asked them if they were still interested in proceeding with the application. If they said no, I would keep the pages we filled out for several months, in case they changed their mind. If they were interested, we proceeded with the paperwork and moved their names up our lists when it was time. Many of them or their families called me to ask how the process was going. When they reached the top of the ready waiting list, and we received notice of an impending vacancy, my resident manager would call the person to make an offer of an apartment. There were times when the staff knew that a resident would be trouble from the first moment, but we had to follow the regulations. Because a person was mean was not a reason we could reject an applicant.

For some senior buildings, the procedure is to have you fill out an application and return it to the staff before you come for the interview. For some places, you have to pay to be on the waiting list. You should understand what each building requires.

Anxiety, Anger, and Excitement

It is normal to feel a bit anxious about making a change, a bit angry about growing old, and a bit excited about possibly moving to a new adventure. How should you prepare for the interview? You should think about what you would like in an apartment or a new environment. You should come to the interview with a list of questions. Write down the answers. Like in a doctor's office, you might not understand or remember what is being said. Ask plenty of questions. You should ask about levels of care and expectations the staff has. You should also know what financial obligations you would have. Ask what your exact monthly costs would be, what services that would include, and what extra services you might be able to have. You also want to know when the rents, food costs, or other fees will be changed and what the average monthly or yearly increases have been. Ask the interviewer to clarify technical terms with which you are not familiar.

Eighteen Questions You Should Ask at the Interview
1. What are the good points about this facility?
2. What are the bad points about this facility?
3. How old is this building?
4. Do I meet the financial requirements?
5. Do I meet the physical requirements?
6. What will my apartment or room look like?
7. What kind of meal program do you offer?
8. How much will it cost me to live here each month?
9. What if I do not want to participate in the meal program?
10. How large a staff is there?
11. What kind of care will I receive?
12. What activities do you offer?

13. What are the rules about coming and going and having visitors and pets?
14. When would I be able to move in?
15. What happens on move-in day?
16. What am I allowed to bring?
17. Who will decide when I have to move out of here?
18. Would I be happy here?

What Your Answers Should Be

For any questions asked of you, your answers should be honest ones. If you do not remember an answer, it is fine to write down the question and tell the interviewer that you will get back to him. No one is expected to know all the answers. You should feel at the end of the interview that you were treated well, that you understand the requirements for living in the facility, and what will happen from that day on in regard to the application process. You probably will be asked to sign many papers at the interview, but not one of those should be that you are obligated to move. Most of the signatures give the staff the necessary permission to continue the application process.

I remember an interview with a couple for whom English was not their native language. I told them that I would go slowly and geared my talk so that they seemed to understand. They were still confused, and when their son was invited into the office, he noted their discomfort, and yelled at me for not speaking to them in a way they could understand. I went through the process again in front of him. He was not so angry at me when he realized that it was not really a language issue, that they were just not appropriate candidates for independent living.

If It Is Not the Right Place

It might not be the right building for you or the right level of care. You have to accept the interviewer's conclusion or go through their appeal process, but in the end, it really may not be the right place for you, or the regulations plainly prohibit you from living there. Go to several places for tours and interviews. Come for lunch or dinner to try it out. Stay for some of the activities. Talk to the residents. You cannot like everything about a place, but you should feel that you could live comfortably there. Then you should think about it for a few days or weeks before you make up your mind to continue the application process. Now is the time that you should use both the rational and the emotional sides of your brain to discuss if this place is appropriate and why.

As it is said, honesty really is the best policy. One of the saddest interviews I conducted was when a woman was brought to our facility by her son. She was told by him that she was going "on an outing" to see some places in the area. Since I always interviewed the applicant alone for the first few minutes, I asked her why she wanted to move here. It was our policy to have the applicant express her opinion about moving. She said she did not want to move, she is perfectly happy where she is, and she did not even know that this was an application interview. When I questioned the son, he explained that had he told his mother where they were going, she would have been too upset.

I explained to her the pros and cons about moving to our facility. She then felt more comfortable, but she still adamantly did not want to move. The son's point of view was that she really could not stay any longer on her own.

The resolution was poignant. When the woman got up from the chair in my office, we all saw a wet urine stain. It was obvious from her answers to questions and her inability to control her bodily functions or even to admit there was a problem that she was unable to live in our facility for the independent well-elderly.

How the Interviews Should Not Go

My experience from the other side of the desk was with my own parents. When they were in their late seventies, they decided that they would look at several independent living facilities near where I live. My mother thought that my father was failing physically and certainly needed to give up driving. They came to the decision to move to a senior building when some of their friends did. It reminded us of teenage peer pressure. During the time I took them to interviews over the course of three days, I was not acting as the director. I was on the other side of the desk, as the daughter. But I did make a mental list of things I did not like in some of the buildings. Staff showed apartments that were empty or dirty. They did not introduce my parents to other residents in the elevator or to other building workers. They ignored one of my parents in explaining things, or they made poor eye contact. They did not ask our needs. They did not shake hands with the potential resident first and then their family member. Some could not find their names on the lists when I called ahead to confirm their appointments. Some treated our questions as though they were stupid instead of treating them as important to ask and to be answered. One director should have tidied up her office for our interview. She had a Maalox bottle on her desk. The message from these examples is that you and your relatives should be treated with respect at each facility, and if you are not, you should consider this poor attitude as a reflection on the facility.

My father did not feel ready to move, and he did not like the first few places. I asked him what he wanted in an apartment building. He said, using his poetic imagination and reacting to the institutional look of several of the places we had already visited, that he wanted to see dappled sunlight reflected through lace curtains. I thought that he would never move. But when we were at the very next place, which was the last one on my list, we were seated in the lobby waiting for the interview. I glanced down at the rug and saw dappled sunlight shining through the lace curtains. I pointed it out to him, and we both knew that this was the place. The fact that it was a five-minute drive from my house was only icing on the cake. Sometimes you just get lucky in this complicated and emotional process.

Keys for Seniors:
- Come with a list of your own questions.
- Write down the answers.
- Make sure you have covered the Eighteen Questions You Should Ask at the Interview.
- Ask for information in writing, so you can refer to it after the interview.
- It is normal to feel a bit anxious at the interview, a bit angry about growing old, and a bit excited about possibly moving to a new adventure.
- Understand what your financial obligations would be.
- Check that all application forms have been properly signed, and get copies.
- Sample the meals and activities they offer.
- Use both the rational and emotional sides of your brain to discuss if this place is appropriate.
- Do not feel rushed into making a decision about moving in there.
- At the end of the interview, you should feel that you were treated with respect, that you understand the requirements, and that you know what will happen from now on.

Keys for Adult Children:

- When you start the interview process, make sure your parent's name is on all the waiting lists of appropriate facilities.
- Realize that your parent is the main person at the interview.
- Understand the levels of care this place offers to make certain it is right for your parent.
- If it is not the right place, ask for other options and recommendations.
- Get information in writing, so you can refer to it after the interview.
- Make sure you have covered the Eighteen Questions You Should Ask at the Interview.
- Know if your parent can meet the financial obligations of the facility.
- Check that all application forms have been properly signed, and get copies.
- Ask for a floor plan of the unit for which your parent qualifies.
- Sample the meals and activities they offer.
- Use both the rational and emotional sides of your brain to discuss if this place is appropriate.
- At the end of the interview, you should feel that you were treated with respect, that you understand the requirements, and that you know what will happen from now on.

Chapter 6
Downsizing

"I Don't Have a Clue"

Once you have decided to make the move to a senior facility, that means you have to downsize, to choose what will go to the new place. It is a difficult and sometimes overwhelming task, one that is better done if you have some help. Ideally, you and your family should work together to make this transition easier. The moving process is more than calling a mover and setting a date. You should start with taking inventory of your emotional state and your physical environment. Call a family meeting, and have this talk:

The Big Six Downsizing Questions
1. What will I miss about my old place?
2. What will I not miss about my old place?
3. What should I take to my new place?
4. What will I like about my new place?
5. What will I not like about my new place?
6. Who will do what in the moving process?

Dividing Up the Moving Tasks

When you put in perspective the elements of the move, you will be better able to cope with it. It is also helpful for each relative to have his assignment. One may get estimates from moving companies. One may contact a realtor to start the sale process. One may be in charge of getting tape and boxes and starting to load them. One may organize the yard sale of things you no longer want or need. One may work out the financial obligations you will have in the move and in regard to the new living arrangement. One may get things ready to donate to charity. Or maybe it is one relative who is assigned to do all of these tasks. Or maybe it is you, the one who is moving, who will do them all. If you want to and are able to, that is fine. But it may be a time when there are things you no longer want to do or can do. Be honest in what your capabilities are.

A Time for Introspection

It is a time to talk with each other about what you can now do. It is also a good time for introspection, to validate what you have done in the past. This process will give you an anchor to yourself, because what has been familiar to you is drifting away.

A good mental exercise is for you to write a poem. Now for those of you who think you cannot do this, I have seen interesting and revealing poems written in the following manner. Have someone say, "What do you feel at your age?" You answer, "At my age, I feel..." The questioner should write down the sentence starting with At my age, I feel. You should repeat the question and answer at least ten times. At then end, you have a free verse poem that should give insight into you at this time of your life. You can write another poem in the same manner. This one is called "I Love You When..." This one works well for all three generations to make their list, which does not rhyme, but which is a poem because of its rhythmic repetition. A third poem can be written by having someone say, "Throughout your lifetime, what did your hands do?" Each answer should start out with "My hands..." The depth of thought in these easy-to-write poems may startle you.

How did we go from not having a clue about how to downsize your home to writing poems? It is because this is a time of introspection. As we take inventory of our environment, we should also take inventory of ourselves. It is stressful to move at any time, but this time it is compounded, because you are experiencing the loss of some parts of who you were and are concerned about the prospect of giving up much of what you have. So since you will have to give up so much of your belongings for your move, you should take the time to validate yourself.

Frustration and Patience

What the adult children can get frustrated about is multiplied during this intimidating time of moving. Maybe they do not realize the attachment you have to a certain item or piece of clothing. If you tell them that this one is what you wore when you got engaged or this one is what you found on the beach during a happy family vacation, they will better understand why you want to keep these items. Also during their frustrations, they need to remember to have patience about repeating things to you. Maybe you did not hear it in the first place or you did not process it or did not remember it. They also need to decide when to say that you already told them that story. They need to know that you are not doing these things to annoy them on purpose, that this is how you process things lately. Of course, it is up to you to put your best foot forward, like making sure you are wearing the correct hearing aids with batteries that are working that day and every day.

The most dramatic downsizing contrast I observed during my years in senior housing was the couple who had lived in a mansion for decades while he was a business success. Then for a number of reasons, he lost the business and the house and was forced to apply for subsidized housing. The only remnant of their life from years ago was their luxury car, so old that it was no longer worth anything in a trade-in, but still working. It was the fanciest car in the parking lot of Filbert Gardens. Maybe your downsizing will not be as stark a contrast, but nonetheless it will still be difficult.

Grieving About Moving

By the time you reach the age of thinking about senior living, you are not a stranger to loss and to the accompanying grieving. We have been taught that the steps in the grieving process are denial, anger, bargaining, depression, and then acceptance. To relate these steps to moving to a senior living facility, you arrive at the decision from varying places on this list. You may feel isolation and depression in your current place. You may experience anger that you are not as young or capable as you once were or that your children are pushing you to move. You may be in denial that there is any problem with your current living situation. However, the reality is that you will come to the acceptance of your new circumstance at some point. I have seen people move into a senior building still in denial, still angry, still depressed, but the forced socialization defeats the isolation and over time lessens the grief. You also have both public and private levels of grief. That means that what you tell people you are upset about may only be the tip of the iceberg of what is really making you grieve. Some people work out their grief by talking about the situation. Some never work it out. Some find it helpful to share the memories of that person or that place. It is normal to mourn your losses, but adapting to the new situation gives you a more healthy perspective.

So grieving the loss of your own home or apartment and the freedom that it produced is expected. Three suggestions to help you move through the grieving process and make the move easier for you are to make your own decisions about what should be moved, to take a memory from each room, and to implement closure ceremonies.

Deciding What to Take

First, get involved in the moving process. You can study the floor plan of your new place to decide what furniture to take or what new items you will need to purchase. If you are moving to a group home, assisted living facility, or a nursing home, you will have to find out what you are supposed to bring with you. If your decision is to stay in your current place, it is now an appropriate time to decide what furniture you should keep and what you should not keep. You want to make your place as safe as possible, so maybe creating wider passageways means that you no longer have room for that end table. You may also want to get a reclining chair that can lift you upward to help you get out of the chair more easily. Look at each piece of furniture with a critical eye, asking yourself if you need it anymore or if it should be replaced.

Closets and cupboards are definitely a problem. You probably are not moving to a place that has more storage space than you had. So now is the time to give away things you have not worn or used in the last year or things that no longer fit. It is also the time to weed out what you no longer need in your collection of bed linens and towels. For kitchen items and dishes, think about what your needs will be. If there is a meal or meals served for you in your new place, then you will not be doing any or as much cooking as you once did. Decide what you will need for entertaining, and then cut that amount in half. Chances are that you will want to be taken out to a restaurant with your family or guests, so you probably will not need the baking pans and serving platters.

You may want to employ a certified senior move manager, who can organize, pack, and unpack what you would like to take to your new place. This professional should make this difficult process easier for you by giving you guidance and by listening to you. To help you locate one in your area, you can look at the website from the National Association of Senior Move Managers at www.nasmm.com.

The American Moving and Storage Association at www.moving.org has a "Top 10 List for a Smooth Move," which is summarized here:

1. Get at least three written estimates. Be sure to show the mover all that will be moved, including things in your attic, basement, garage, storage area, and shed. Choose one of the estimates that is in the middle of the range, not the high or low one.

2. Make sure you get and read the three pre-move required documents from the mover. They should be about your rights and responsibilities, about getting ready to move, and about the company's arbitration program.

3. Don't give the moving company a large down payment.

4. Be sure to have all your questions answered so that you fully understand what will happen and when.

5. If you can move in off-peak season, do so. June to September is the busy season. Always avoid the end of the month. If you must move during the high season, try moving mid-month or mid-week.

6. Give the mover the phone number where you can be reached during the move. You want to avoid storage costs, if possible. Always get the driver's full name, identification number, and truck number, so you can track his location during your move.

7. Do not pack your valuables like cash, coins, jewelry, photographs, and important papers. Take those with you, or send them ahead by means of a traceable service, like FedEx or United Parcel Service.

8. Separate your personal travel items, like the clothes you will need for the duration of the moving time, important documents, and the moving contract. You do not want the mover to put these items on the truck.

9. Remember that in spite of your best plans, things can go wrong. Moving is a time of great stress. You should approach the day with patience and understanding.

10. Use a certified mover. You can find further information at the U.S. Department of Transportation (DOT) and at www.protectyourmove.gov, a website from the Federal Motor Carrier Safety Administration.

Saving a Special Object from Each Room

Secondly, to make your move easier, take one object from each room to your new place. Its size depends on the limitations of the new place, so it could be a clock you received as a wedding present, a coin bank from your dresser, or the souvenir spoon collection you enlarged after each vacation. Choose your favorite artwork and framed photographs that should go with you. Where you are moving should look like a combination of new and familiar. On a practical level, hand-carry a bag on moving day that has in it a snack, all your remote controls, monetary tips for the movers, your tool kit, your medications, a pad of paper and pens to make lists, and a roll of toilet paper.

Having a Closure Ceremony

Thirdly, to ease this transition time, you need closure, that is, ways to say goodbye to people as well as to things. It may be the time you should give up driving, something that may not be so easy to do. When my father stopped driving, we made a celebratory dinner for him to give him closure. We talked about how and where he learned to drive, some of the car trips we took together, and the kinds of cars he owned. You may also want to have a reception or a party to say goodbye to your friends and neighbors. Some of them may want to move as you are doing. You also will have to say goodbye to your neighborhood whose places may have been so important in creating your life memories. Whether it is the local school which you or your children attended or the supermarket or the library, you should have a time to say goodbye. Other ideas are to have a farewell meal at your favorite neighborhood restaurant and visit your local park or movie house one more time. When leaving your former home and entering the new one, you should say some words of importance to you, like a thank you for the years you spent in the old place and a welcome greeting to your new place. Closure is the opposite of opening, which is what you will do at your next home.

Family Involvement and Notifications

It helps to make a list of the specific tasks you need to do or need to assign family members to do. Some of these assignments can be done by family members who live out of town, because they can be done over the phone or over the internet. Both generations should have funds for moving expenses. The adult children should have a visiting fund to pay for unplanned trips and funeral expenses that have not already been pre-paid by your parent. You should make sure to have the proper payment and tips for the movers. Some companies want a cashier's check, and some want cash. Notify your post office of your new address and get their kit for informing others. Cut off your utilities. Notify your magazine and newspaper subscriptions of your new address. Close your bank accounts, and empty your safe deposit box. Call the customer service number for your credit cards to inform them of your new address and that they can expect to see purchases from your new state or neighborhood. Change your voter registration. Have your medical records transferred to your new facility or your new doctors' offices. Arrange to have an extra supply of prescriptions to tide you over until your new doctors have met with you and can begin writing prescriptions. If you own a funeral plot that is far from your new home, you may want to sell the old one and purchase a new plot. Or you may want to keep the one you have because it is next to your spouse or other family members. Just make your wishes known to your family. If you are moving out of state, you will need to get a new driver's license. This move may mark the proper time to give up your driver's license and get instead an ID card from the Department of Motor Vehicles. The documents you need for these transactions differ from state to state, so make sure you know what to bring to get your new document.

Your old place is now empty. It is normal to feel sadness. But there is the arrival to which you can now look forward. You are taking with you the memories from your former home. The raising of your family and the ups and downs of life and job are all there. It is time for the next chapter of your life. This one was about moving out. Now you are ready to move in.

Keys for Seniors:
- Downsizing provides you with a time for introspection to validate what you have done in the past, and to give you an anchor to yourself, as what has been familiar to you is drifting away.
- Topics for your validating poems are "At My Age," "I Love You When," and "My Hands."
- As you take inventory of your environment, take inventory of yourself.
- The steps in the grieving process are similar to what you may feel in the moving process.
- Take a memory from each room in your old house to put in the new place.
- Have a closure ceremony when you leave your former home.
- Close accounts, and give notice of your move.
- On moving day, hand-carry a bag that has in it a snack, all your remote controls, monetary tips for the movers, your tool kit, your medications, and a roll of toilet paper.
- Have an extra supply of your prescriptions that can tide you over until you meet with your new doctors.
- Switch your sadness at leaving your home to the excitement of moving into a new place.

Keys for Adult Children:
- Downsizing provides your parent with a time for introspection to validate his accomplishments and to give him an anchor during this unsettling time.
- Help your parent validate himself by asking him the leading questions so he can write the poems of "At My Age," "I Love You When," and "My Hands."
- During these frustrating times, have patience when you need to repeat yourself.
- Help formulate a closure ceremony to make the moving an easier transition.
- Give out-of-town siblings some moving tasks that can be done over the phone or the internet.
- Help with setting up appointments with new doctors and filling the new prescriptions.
- Understand your parent's sadness at leaving the old and his anticipation about the new.

Chapter 7
Moving In

"I Don't Remember"

The worst moving in experience we saw at Filbert Gardens was the couple who arrived with two suitcases, deposited them in their apartment, and came down to sit in the lobby. After awhile, the husband and wife came to the front desk and said that they decided they do not like it at this hotel and that they wanted to check in to another hotel. Either they did not remember that they were moving in or their daughter was never fully honest with them. After the moving van arrived and unloaded their belongings, they commented that this hotel had good service. Eventually, they understood that they were going to live in this building, and they succeeded in making a positive transition. It is sometimes hard to tell what people have been told, what they remember from the interview, and what they want to remember. It often takes patience on the part of both the staff and the family to help with the transition to a new living environment.

First Observations

So what do you first see when you arrive at your new place? Sometimes it is the people who sit in chairs in the lobby. Critics say that they make the place look depressing. Others view them as those who may be no longer capable of going out of the building on their own. Their world has become smaller, but they are determined to get out of their apartments, to make a connection with each other and with their neighbors. They enjoy watching the comings and goings of friends, families, and staff. After you are settled, you might want to join them and start a conversation.

Family as Worker Bees and Parent as Queen Bee

I have observed how adult children can be most helpful during the move and the setting up of the new place. Instead of the family members saying, "I don't remember" pertaining to the building procedures, they should ask many questions, read all that was provided prior to and at the move, and be cognizant of the move-in rules and times and days of elevator use. The family can be the worker bees, while the parent is the queen bee. They can run the errands to buy new items that were not part of the move or that are needed now. One resident upon move-in said she could not find her vacuum cleaner, and her daughter said that is because her mother threw it away at the old apartment because she did not think she had much longer to live. They went out to buy a new one that day, and she lived in the building for many more years.

    The adult children and grandchildren can hang the picture but should do so where the parent wants it hung. They can arrange the clothing in the closets, but in the order the parent desires. They can make suggestions about which drawer should hold which kitchen utensil, but the final decision is up to the parent, the one who will be living there. They can suggest that this is a good time to buy new bathroom towels, but the color selection should be up to the parent. They can make a map of the nearest markets, banks, beauty and barber shops, cleaners, and malls. They can break down the moving cartons and take them to the place designated in the house rules. They actually should read the handbook for new residents, to serve as a resource when their parent has a question. They should introduce themselves to the staff and make sure the front desk person has all the proper emergency contacts. They can get an extra key to the front door and to the apartment, if that is all right with the parent. They can also chat with neighbors to see what people enjoy doing and what they might have in common with their parent. They can ask the parent for a shopping list and then go to the supermarket to buy the items. They should add a favorite food that is not on the list and a bouquet of flowers or a plant, in order to brighten the new surroundings. Whether you call or visit your parent once a day or once a week or less frequently, you are establishing and maintaining the lines of communication. One son of a resident of Filbert Gardens did his mother's laundry at his home. She reciprocated by making him an oatmeal breakfast twice a week. You do what works for the two of you.

In regard to adult children who have siblings living out of the area, here are some suggestions. Set up times to have web camera chats with the parent. Send them photos of the new place or the redone home or apartment. Forward to them copies of the emergency contacts, including doctors' phone numbers and medication list. Also, give them copies of the general power of attorney, the living will, the durable power of attorney for health care, and the funeral arrangements or requests. Tell them what problems you are having. They may have a solution and may appreciate being let in on the problem. For those who have siblings who are cut off or who have no siblings, try to incorporate a friend as a helper for you as you try to manage. I was a helper to a friend when he went on vacation. I was to be the contact for his dog in the pet hotel and his mother in the senior building. He gave me instructions of what to do if I received certain phone calls from the staff members of either of these facilities. Fortunately, I did not get a call from either place, but I was so afraid that when he returned from vacation, I would have gotten my signals crossed and his mother would be wearing the red and white bandana and his dog would be using a walker.

Mind and Body Workouts After Moving

On move-in day, you may hear people complaining about the building, the food, the staff, their families, or each other. Then you ask yourself, "Why did I not hear them when I came for the interview? Did I make a mistake in moving here? Will I hate it here?" You might, but it is too soon to know yet. Remember that some residents are simply complainers by nature. Probably you will hate some of the things and like some others, just like it was in the home you recently left.

You actually may be so stimulated by this move that you feel better physically. You are certainly giving your brain a workout in learning about the new place and the new procedures. Researchers say in regard to your brain that you should use it or lose it. A move is an exercise for your brain and body, as well as an emotional roller coaster.

Taking Some R and R: Rest and Regrouping

After you have experienced the enormous stress levels of breaking down a home and moving, then setting up a new home, you should give yourself a few weeks of R and R, that is, rest and regrouping. I did have one resident who moved in on a Sunday, and by Monday morning when I went to her apartment to welcome her, it looked as though she had lived there forever. Everything was in place, all pictures were hung, and she even had organized her closets. She was an exception. The usual scenario is that you walk around cartons for several weeks or at least until the family can come back to help you get things in order.

It is a good idea to plan where furniture and other belongings will go in the new place when you are packing up the old place. But you will have to be flexible when you see that some item may not fit where you had wanted it to be. While you are unpacking, you may find a picture of yourself in front of the Eiffel Tower and blurt out, "Was I there?" As you go through other memorabilia, you might not remember where you purchased some of the things. Eventually, if your memory is on a decline, you may get to the point when you have to ask what to do with that same object.

Laughing at the Mess Around You and the Mess in Your Head

Take time to laugh at the mess around you and the mess in your head. Once your surroundings get in order, your mind will feel less cluttered. But then you will realize once again that your memory may not be what it used to be. It is a good time to think of this old joke. The woman went up to her pastor after the sermon and said, "I know just what you are saying when you tell us it is time to think about the hereafter. I am at the point now that when I go into a room, I look around blankly and say, 'What am I here after?'"

So take it easy for the first few weeks, but try not to

isolate yourself during this transition time. It is the reason that a mandatory communal meal is such a good idea. You are expected to come to dinner each night, so you have to get yourself together enough to find your way to the dining room or to be met by your volunteer neighbor escort for the first few days and then to socialize.

Learning About the New Place

Instead of the new resident saying, "I don't remember what to do," he should be learning the rules and customs at the new place. We had a lady who told new residents that the toaster in the snack bar did not work on Wednesdays. What she really meant by that comment was that the resident who volunteered there on Wednesdays did not know how to work the toaster and therefore did not use it on her day volunteering there. So people learned to order toast on other days of the week and that the day she was there, she did make a great tuna salad platter.

It is important to familiarize yourself with the procedures for a fire and a fire drill. Know what you should do when the fire alarm sounds or where you should go to pull an alarm in case you see the fire. In Filbert Gardens, there was a firewall between each apartment and in between floors. So if there were to be a fire, only the floor where it was and the ones above it and below it for good measure had to be evacuated. The staff had a chart for the fire personnel that told which residents were unable to walk down the flights of steps and so would have to be transported by emergency workers. Within your apartment, make sure your sprinkler is not covered. One of our residents had a parakeet he let fly around the apartment, so he put a covering over the sprinkler, barring the bird from landing on it. The alarm bell should be loud enough for you to hear without your hearing aid, or you should have the management company install a flashing alarm signal to meet your needs. In three decades at Filbert Gardens, there was only one small fire, and it was confined to one unit. But we had frequent fire drills, so staff and residents would know how to react. We also demonstrated to groups of residents each month how to operate the emergency telephone in the elevator, in case they were stuck and needed to call for assistance.

In your learning about the building, you may hear things like these snippets that my residents said or reported hearing. They add to the flavor of your new home. Some women lined up to get a whiff, because they heard that a man who smells nice was moving in. A woman moved in to be near her sister, who died the next week. Another woman moved in to help her handicapped brother, and she died before he did. Someone's husband had a stroke on the way to moving in. Certainly, all of their lives changed more than they were expecting. One couple wanted to return to Florida no matter what the family or staff did. They did not go back, because they had sold that home and finally admitted that they needed the supportive services this building provided. There was a woman who was the oldest resident at the time and told us that we could say someone there was 98 but not point her out. She did not look a day over 88. People used their ages in different ways, and you will observe how people react to their ages. Some are proud of the years they have achieved but bemoan their current and future limitations. One lady told the gardening speaker that she could not repot her plant, because she was 93 years old. The fact that she could bring it down to the activity room and take care of her other plants in her apartment did not matter to her. She drew the line at repotting. When I asked another woman if she could volunteer for a project, she said that she was not as well as she looked.

We had one resident who acted as a self-appointed greeter to newcomers by singing their favorite songs to them. He actually found out that many of the newcomers went to his high school in Brooklyn. We had several who would steal toilet paper from the lobby restrooms, because they were in constant fear that their money would run out and they therefore would not be able to get their own toilet paper. Some call this an example of the Depression mentality, wherein people who have lived through the Great Depression in the 1930's still cannot be sure that they will not lose their belongings and money yet again.

Developing Friendships

As you are becoming more acquainted with the building and its people, you may be surprised at how friendships develop. Some people never made friends, or they actually alienated others. However, there were some interesting cases. We had a man who was severely bent over from his spine degeneration, and when people first saw him, they walked away. But when they started to talk to him, many realized he was a sparkling conversationalist and soon looked beyond his physical appearance. Some of those friendships may even lead to romance in the building. One man was smitten with a dinner table mate. One came to his interview crying about his loneliness now that his wife had died, but was taking out a woman resident within a week of moving in. They married each other but kept their two separate apartments.

Successful Staff

You should also learn about some of the issues with which the staff deals. The building director wants keep the building filled, but she has to adhere to federal, state, local, and company regulations. She has to tell some people that they are just not appropriate for this particular building. On the other hand, she may admit people you do not think should live there. But just because they use walkers or wheelchairs and the building is meant to be for the independent elderly does not mean that these residents are not independent in their own ways. You may hear, "We never had people with walkers before. This place is starting to look like a nursing home." But the admission criteria may mandate that they have to be able to take care of themselves or direct someone to take care of them. There are levels upon levels of regulations. Having difficulty walking does not necessarily mean that they cannot otherwise care for themselves. Senior buildings are places where people experience mental and physical declines and are dealing with dementia, shingles, cataracts, broken hips, heart attacks, and strokes. But they are also filled with people who are trying to make the best of their health situations.

As the building director, I had to do some unusual things to keep the building running smoothly. I had to cancel the future showing of the movie, "Oh! Calcutta!", because our volunteer resident thought it was a travelogue about India and did not realize there was nudity that may be offensive to his neighbors. I had to oversee the moving of a resident to a lower floor of the high-rise building, because she was a chain smoker who tended to fall asleep in her easy chair, and the fire truck ladders could not reach to the original floor where she lived. We put her in an apartment on the second floor and treated her clothes and chair with fire retardant solutions. I also had to station myself near a lobby restroom, because for several days someone was leaving it dirty and unsanitary. I watched for what I thought was a long time and did not catch the guilty party, proving the twist on the adage that a watched potty never soils. Eventually, we found the woman, who really needed to move to a facility that offered a higher level of care. I also had to call our building engineer, requesting that the newly delivered dumpster be removed. He said that we needed it for some renovation. I agreed but said that we did not need one with a nude painted on the side of the dumpster he could not see from his office window.

So much of being a successful staff in a senior building, or being a relative of an aging senior for that matter, involves patience, empathy, and the three B's—not Bach, Beethoven, and Brahms, but: be accessible, be accountable, and be pleasant. The staff of your facility should show patience when people repeat things. Daily, we have to deal with the complaints and the problems and even the compliments. One charming compliment was paid to me when I asked a resident how she felt. Her answer was that she was better now that she saw me. There certainly are highs and lows in being a director of a senior building. A woman gave me an inadvertent compliment through her slip of the tongue. She called to discuss an issue with me and then said something like "as long as I have you on the throne..." However, I was soon reminded of the difficulties of the job when we invited a police officer to speak to a resident meeting about street safety. He had a hard time controlling the audience. He pulled me aside, and with his gun, handcuffs, and badge gleaming in the sunlight, said to me that I have such a hard job.

Understanding Concepts of Aging

The staff in your building should understand the changes aging brings. I found that an excellent staff training exercise that is used in some hospitals and senior centers is a trading places experience. Staff members sit in a wheelchair. They will see how much their neck gets strained just by having to look up at people's faces. They learn that they should kneel down to speak to a person in a wheelchair. The other parts of the exercise involve putting on glasses that are too strong a prescription for them or covering plain glasses with Vaseline to see what someone with limited vision sees. They also try to walk with weights on their ankles or with their knees tied together. They come to realize that it is not easy to function with such limitations and that their parents will be like this one day and that another day before they know it, they may have these limitations. With their understanding the lessons of this experience, they can be more helpful to the residents and to their own aging relatives.

Communal Meals

You do not need to be reminded of the loss of your five senses, but the researchers have concluded that two-thirds of taste is from smell, and that almost 50 percent of seniors have lost their full sense of smell. You will dine with people who hate the food because either it is bad or they are angry that they are no longer capable of preparing meals the way they used to do. Or perhaps they can no longer smell and hence taste the flavors of the food. If you do not like the food, there are some positive steps you can take. Arrange a tour of the kitchen. I have sent residents and their family members to meet with the cooks, to see how dedicated they are, to observe what spices they add to the food, and to offer their own recipes. I have had residents who used to work in restaurants give suggestions and those who were former waiters give pep talks to our wait staff. I have also seen residents bring their own condiments to the table, because they know that they like their meals spicier or with a certain herb. It gives them a bit more control. This feeling of loss of control, especially for a woman who has cooked all her life and now cannot or does not, is a reminder of one more thing that is gone or has been taken from her. I tried to emphasize that since we only served one meal a day, she could still work her kitchen magic on her other meals or special baked treats. But more often than not, she was no longer physically able to be the cook she once was and needed to mourn that loss.

We have often heard that the food tastes better when the family is visiting. This situation is a case of more enjoyment being added to the meal experience and to the sense of anticipation. I urge families to sample the food. We eat with my mother at her independent living facility about once a month and find the food tasty and nutritious. I also like that where she lives, the staff contacts residents who have not come to the meal that day. This system is a good way to make sure you are all right. The dining room problem of poor service is an issue related to rate of pay and therefore retention of staff. On the one hand, residents are entitled to proper service at their tables, but on the other hand, they are there also for the socialization. So if they have to spend a little longer at the meal, maybe that is not such a bad thing. Certainly, if the dining room service is poor, that matter should be discussed with the management staff. On another note, I feel that music should not be played in a senior citizen dining room, because it is an interference to those whose hearing is diminished, and for those who wear hearing aids, they have trouble differentiating between background music and voices in front of them.

Exceeding Expectations

These losses of yours are compounded in the new place. You feel the loss of things that were once important to you, the people, places, and objects. But there is the cliché of the glass half empty or half full. It is your opportunity to view this new situation as half full. People certainly do better in this transition time when they have a positive attitude. So it should be not what you no longer have, but what you do now have. This philosophy forms the basis of the regrouping you should afford yourself. What am I still capable of doing here? What do I want to try to do that I never did or was putting off until a more convenient time? The staff and your family all hope that you make a smooth transition to your new surroundings. You probably hope the same thing. You can remember that original talk you had with your family about your fears and frustrations about staying in your home. By moving to a place with a higher level of care or adding those levels of care to your original home, you should be experiencing greater security and comfort. That was probably on the list of expectations from your family.

For the 20th anniversary of Filbert Gardens, I interviewed half the residents, some of whom wanted to move in originally and some of whom did not. Here are several of their comments, with their permission, describing what they enjoyed about living there:

After living alone for a few years, I find myself in great happiness living here.

This is a haven of good people who have come from near and far to be close to their children and relatives for the most part. In general, everyone is friendly and tries to make the most and the best of their new home. In addition, Filbert Gardens also plays a very important part in providing excellent programs for our interest and our pleasure. This is proven by the attendance and cooperation of our Filbert Gardens family. The staff also plays a big part in keeping everyone happy and informed of all activities. If I have painted a pretty picture, that was my intention, and I can only add God bless Filbert Gardens, its staff, and its residents.

The place is immaculate. When you walk into the Trash Room, it glistens, and you get "house conscious." You feel you have to go back to clean your own kitchen floor. They keep you happy all day long with lectures, movies, and wonderful entertainment. Our surveys always come out the best, because we go out of our way to keep everyone happy. Filbert Gardens is like a family. You are never alone. If you get tired of television, you can always go down and find people. You are going to love it here the way I do. Just have long, healthy, happy years here.

After my wife died, for about three years, I lived like a hermit. My family asked me to move here, and now I have a family of 250 people residing here. I am not a hermit anymore.

I try to be helpful to those who need help. I like to know that people are okay. We walk together outside. Friendliness is the name of the game.

It is like a second home to us. Everybody is nice, including the staff. I have been here seven years.

We are happy to be with a lot of people, and I met a nice girlfriend.

I am very happy here. I feel protected, and I am near my family.

I enjoy the outside, which is kept extremely well. When I came here five years ago, I made friends and still maintain the same ones. I look forward to meeting the newcomers, also.

It is great. We would like to spend another 68 years together here.

I enjoy living here because although you live alone, you are never isolated in any way.

I am glad I made the change to be among people, and I have very many friends here.

I like the fact that I feel safe in my apartment.

I am happy that our son brought us here.

When I came here, I met someone who lived across the hall from me in Pittsburgh thirty-seven years ago.

I like playing pool here with the younger generation.

I enjoy not having to cook and not having to go shopping.

I enjoy meeting all kinds of people from different backgrounds and having conversations with them. I also enjoy the variety of programming and the classes here. I feel like I am back in college again.

I could have asked these same people what they did not like and may have had a longer list. But the point is that some of these people wanted to move, and some did not. They made the transition to senior living the best they could. They have limitations, failing health of body and mind, but they have tried. They did something, and they were proud to say what they enjoyed about senior living.

Keys for Seniors:
- Making a transition to this new place takes patience.
- The family can be the worker bees, while the parent is the queen bee.
- Send photos of your new place to your relatives and friends.
- A move is an exercise for your brain and body, as well as an emotional roller coaster.
- You should give yourself a few weeks of R and R, rest and regrouping.
- Take time to laugh at the mess around you and the mess in your head.
- Try not to isolate yourself at first.

- Have an open mind and mouth in regard to the food.
- In your regrouping of your abilities, have a positive attitude.

Keys for Adult Children:
- It takes patience on the part of the staff and the family to help with the transition to a new place.
- Learn about the move-in rules and use of elevator during that day.
- The family can be the worker bees, while the parent is the queen bee.
- You can help with the hanging of the pictures, but your parent should decide where he wants them to hang.
- Do the first shopping and include a favorite food that is not on the list and a bouquet of flowers or a plant.
- To help siblings who live out of town, set up web camera chats with them and your parent.
- Have patience and empathy.
- Follow the three B's: be accessible, be accountable, and be pleasant.
- The food may taste better when the family is visiting.
- Listen to what the other residents are saying, and emphasize the positive to your parent.

Chapter 8
Acclimating

"I Love It Here"

So how can you learn to enjoy where you have moved? How do you acclimate? Here is a composite vignette of four dinner table mates at Filbert Gardens discussing where they came from and what they did when they arrived there to make it feel like their home.

Coming Together

The dining room table near the window was always a hotbed of discussion. Tim and Louise were the conservatives of the group, while Olga and Charles were the liberals. Each night at dinner, they argued about an article from the newspaper. Tim always went back to the fact that during his childhood, he was allowed to play in the neighborhood from after breakfast until sunset. His parents never locked their doors, and they centered their life around the small town activities in Iowa. When he finished high school and enlisted in the army, he was sent to Europe in the waning years of the war. Upon his return, he married Louise and worked as an accountant until his retirement. He and Louise disagreed about moving to a senior building. She was tired of cooking, but he loved to work in his garden and did not want anyone to annoy him. Louise centered her life around her volunteer activities in her neighborhood, school, and church. She was tired of running activities and of volunteering for committees. All she wanted to do was relax and say "no" when asked to do something. She had heard about Filbert Gardens when they were visiting their son and he said that his friend's mother recently moved in. When they came to the interview, Tim said that he would not move unless he could do what he wanted to here, and Louise said that she did not want to do anything here. I told them that they had to follow the rules of apartment living, but what they chose to do was up to them. She wandered one day into the computer room and sat in on a class. Within two months, she was emailing her grandchildren and helping to make posters advertising building events. He presented to the staff a plan to turn a section of the lawn into a vegetable garden and soon was reaping tomatoes. On this night, Tim and Louise were engaged in a heated dinner debate over the future of Social Security.

On the other side of the discussion were Olga and Charles. She was widowed over thirty years ago and raised her two daughters by herself. She was a teacher, and in the days before professional childcare, she had put together a system of before- and after-school classes and activities for her children that enabled her to continue working at her job. She also volunteered with the League of Women Voters and in several presidential and local campaigns. She had a stroke three years ago and decided that she should give up her home and move to a place where she felt safer. When she saw Charles on his move-in day, she invited him to join them at their dinner table. She made the transition to communal living easily, because she had always been a joiner and sampled each activity until she settled on the ones she liked. Charles did not think anything was wrong with where he lived until his son visited and saw that his dad was only eating toast and cottage cheese each meal of each day. He convinced Charles to take a look at Filbert Gardens and to sample a dinner during his tour. When Charles thought about making the move, he realized that since he was a life-long union man, maybe he could use his organizational skills to get the residents to stop their complaining about their bodies, which he called their organ recitals, and begin to help out each other. Upon move-in, he became the floor captain and helped to run the Good Night Card Program, making sure residents put out a card on their door knob each night and brought it back in when they woke up. If the card was still on the door by a certain time, he would notify the office, and the staff would check on that resident.

Now, their Social Security discussion teetered back and

forth, with Tim saying that the fund will run out before his children will be eligible and that it is not a viable government program any more. Olga said that she would not be able to afford her living expenses without the checks she receives. The point is that these four people from different backgrounds and with different attitudes can sit over dinner and disagree and agree, but still be happy that they made the transition to a senior living place where they can be as active or passive as they desire.

Enlarging Upon Your Lifestyle

The residents have changed their addresses, and they can change or enlarge upon their lifestyles if they would like. Some of the residents of Filbert Gardens attend a senior camp in the mountains and come back tanned and showing off jewelry they made there in arts and crafts class. Some travel on their own or with senior groups like Elderhostel, a company which offers courses throughout the United States and around the world. Some seniors are even hiring skilled nurses or aides to travel with them to help with their care and mobility. If you would like to have a vacation with all three or four generations together, one relatively carefree example is a family reunion cruise, where all the ages of your family can relax as you sightsee together, and the cooking and other arrangements are done for you. A company that specializes in family reunion cruises is the web-based Your Cruise Concierge.

Other residents walk over to the adjacent community

center for classes, lectures, concerts, and plays. A bus also picks up some to take them to a county senior center or to appointments with doctors. Filbert Gardens held the record for the place where the county Bookmobile had the most customers. Whether it was regular books, large print books, or books on tape or CD, the residents made good use of this service.

Since there was also a nursing home on the same grounds, many residents were able to visit spouses and friends who now lived there. They could also take advantage of the low vision and low hearing clinics the nursing home offered. The Filbert Gardens residents also could volunteer at the nursing home. Before I even entered the field of senior living, I used to take my two-year-old daughter to volunteer with me as a Sunshine Visitor, talking to and singing with the residents. She is now a mother and decided to have her daughter's second birthday party at a nursing home near where they now live. She brought singing, dancing, music, and smiles to the faces of those residents, as the staff provided the birthday cake and decorations. The age differences of eight or nine decades were bridged by this loving gesture.

Intergenerational programs are beneficial for both sides of the age span. Most senior places have parties at holiday time, but I always thought that the children should come on a non-holiday to make that day special. We also had a pen pal program with residents answering letters from the local elementary school students. At the middle and the end of the year, the groups met each other and shared stories and laughs.

Trying the Good and the Bad

Many bonds form within the senior community. One that is quite poignant is among the women who have cared for their ailing husbands and then become widows. Immediately, the sisterhood of women who have been through that heart-wrenching experience encircles the grieving widow. Comfort like that made my mother's grief easier to handle after the death of my ailing father.

When a fellow resident dies, it is helpful to have some sort of closure. There are religious rites that help one say goodbye to neighbors, but we at Filbert Gardens would also have a memory hour, where family and friends could join together to share remembrances of the one who recently died.

In a senior residence, good and bad news and gossip travel fast. Several hours after our morning arrival on move-in day for my parents, my father and teenage daughter went to the lobby to get a newspaper. They overheard one lady say to another one after pointing to my father, "You do not want him. He HAS a wife."

Not everyone makes a smooth or pleasant transition to this kind of living arrangement. We had people at Filbert Gardens who constantly wrote to federal and local officials complaining about the food or arguing that the rent should not be raised. Taking that action is their right, and there are procedures building management and officials go through to ensure that everyone is heard. If changes can and should be made, they usually are. With careful listening to the problem stated and the concerns behind that problem, a good director should be able to make changes or soothe feelings. I had successes and failures, as do all directors.

Home with the Range of People

The building houses a wide range of people, so there are the happy and the unhappy residents, the village idiot, the comedian, the thief, the parent paying for his daughter's drug habit, the meanest man, the scariest woman, the hoarder, and the sex pot. There are also the cliques that are reminiscent of high school. It is really like a little city, and just like in a city, there are rules that need to be enforced. These are some examples of the range of residents and circumstances we had at Filbert Gardens. You may have similar situations where you live.

A son wanted his mother to use the steps for exercise, but she could barely walk even using her cane. I had to take him to the staircase with her and have him see that she was no longer capable of using the steps safely.

One man in his eighties was so desirable that women would flock to his apartment to hear him play his piano.

One woman would not volunteer at our snack bar, because she did not want to put the apron over her perfectly-styled hair. I arranged for the snack bar to order an alternative style of apron, and she then volunteered there for many months.

A woman went to another city to help her son who broke his leg and while there, she broke her arm.

One son told me he feels relieved that when he has to tell his father that he has to follow a certain rule of the building, he can say that it is because the director said so. He liked that he did not have to be the "bad guy" in these confrontations with his parent.

Some comments are absurd on the surface, so I had to ask questions to get at what the man really meant when he asked why I make people come down to the lobby to get on the bus. He really wanted to go on some of the trips, but he was afraid that he would miss the bus or that there would not be a seat for him. I showed him how to sign up for the trips and had someone call to remind him of its pending departure if he was not in the bus line at the right time.

One man ignored me when I greeted him in the elevator, but later that day I received a handwritten note from him, in which in his Old World gracious style he explained that he could not say hello back to me in the elevator due to a case of laryngitis.

Our residents could participate in the Retired Senior Volunteer Program (RSVP), which assigned a resident to be a senior aide. This job was a paid position, and one resident served as the right hand person in the activities department. Other residents in this program were assigned to different locations to help with various projects.

Voices Are Heard

Your new home should have a way to hear your voice. We had an active Residents Association, which was a partner in the management of the building. I met regularly with the president and the group to tell them what the management company was doing and to hear what they were doing and what their needs were. This teamwork and direct communication helped in the smooth running of the building. The resident officers were some people who had always been active in organizations and some who were volunteering for the first time. That element is one of the positive forces in communal living, the opportunity for you to engage.

You may see more people with broken bones. It is not always clear about the case of a broken hip. If you fall and break it, that is one thing, but if the bone breaks and causes you to fall, that is another. At Filbert Gardens, we had the rule that if someone fell, the staff did not move the person. We would call 911 and wait with the person until professional help arrived. We also had a broken bone from an auto accident when a relative picked up three residents to take them out to lunch. However, he pulled away before the last one was ready. Her leg was still out of the car, and it dragged along until he realized what had happened. It was broken, and we all learned our lesson to make sure everyone in our car is in, seat-belted, and ready to go.

We think we had the area's oldest newspaper delivery person. She was a resident in her late nineties. She could not sleep well and loved to walk, so she would come down at 4:30 each morning, load the stack of newspapers into a cart, and deliver them to the subscribers throughout the ten-story building.

Our head of the food committee hated the food, yet she did not institute any changes or make any suggestions on how to make it taste better. I was always impressed with the expertise of our kitchen staff and offered tours to residents and their families, so they could see what went into the food preparation. When one lady complained about the size of the chicken breasts, I had her and her family see them being seasoned and baked. Some of the complaints about the food are legitimate, and some are because people eat in the dining room every night and get tired of the offerings. But another factor is that for some women, they have defined themselves as being good cooks and food providers for their families. When this action is taken away from them because the communal meal is provided, they can feel useless. For these women, we encouraged them to prepare their favorite dishes for their families when they visit or to do their cooking at their lunchtime.

For many men, their feelings of uselessness come to the surface when they have to give up driving. Once, I had to take away the car of a resident who was still driving, even though his vision and reaction time had faded. His son had called me to ask me to be the "bad guy" to tell his father that he had to stop driving. I made an appointment with the man to meet him at his car. He really did know that it was time to stop driving, but he needed a push. We talked about how he loved to drive. I suggested that he donate this car to a charity. We helped him clear out the trunk of the car, and I had him sit in the front seat one last time. Then he was ready to give me his keys. It was one more resident mad at me for a time, but one more grateful son and many more safer roads.

When we were choosing a new rug for the lobby area, I asked our most vocal resident critic to be the rug tester. Then when her choice was installed, I knew that I would not hear complaints from her.

When the husband of an already mean lady died, I asked her if I could give her a hug. Her reply took me aback, saying if it made me feel better. It would not, so I did not.

One man, who drove to visit his wife in a nursing home, ate lunch with her every day. He would tell me how much he hated their food and enjoyed ours.

One woman asked me to tell her next-door neighbor to stop cooking late into the night. I knew that that lady did not cook anymore, so I gave the problem some thought. I asked the lady if she slept with her windows open. She nodded yes, so then I told her that the cooking smells were from a nearby barbeque restaurant. If she closed her window or came to embrace the aroma, she would not be so disturbed by it.

I never knew what people would say when they came into my office. One lady asked me to find her a man. Another said, in effect, "I am well-educated, so I do not understand why people do not like me." I suggested that instead of telling them all about herself she should search for the sparkle in others, looking at people as diamonds in the rough.

Once, I had to find an actual diamond. A lady came crying to my office. She just returned from her doctor's appointment and went to her apartment to put back on her diamond pendant necklace. It was no longer where she thought she had left it. I went through her thought process and guessed that when she got to the doctor, she realized that she had not taken off the necklace, so she did at that time and put it in her purse. She looked in her purse in my office and could not find it. I asked her permission to look through her purse. I noticed that there was a tear in the purse lining and felt that the necklace had slipped inside the lining. I had her place her hand in that slot, and she retrieved her necklace.

Interacting

When my parents moved into their senior building, they just wanted to get unpacked. They did not really think about interacting with the other residents. But as they started to talk to their neighbors and their dinner table mates, they were intrigued by the caliber of the people, who had come from such interesting backgrounds and who shared spellbinding experiences. My parents slowly sampled the activities and found the ones that interested them. My father became the film impresario, choosing the classic movies to be shown on the in-house channel. He also excelled in the trivia games. My mother, who never painted before, now flourished in the arts and crafts class and then volunteered to edit the newsletter and start a literary magazine. They became popular, because they developed a caring for their neighbors and treated everyone with dignity. As their daughter, I was only concerned that they were situated near me, so I could run over quickly in any emergency or for visits. It was made that much sweeter that they became so involved and told me that they were deeply happy that they made the move.

Their feelings are more common than not. Of course, in every senior living facility there are residents for whom nothing is right, ever. But for many who moved in with a negative attitude, we as staff and as family enjoyed watching the transitions to "it really is not as bad as I thought" or to "I love it here." I have given you a sampling of incidents that occur in an independent living building. How you adjust to a move has a great deal to do with your background, your energy, and your abilities. As did Tim, Louise, Olga and Charles at their dinner table, you will adjust to this new setting depending on your personality and your stamina.

Conversation Icebreakers

So when you move in, you may hear the topics of conversation that can range from joys or disappointments with the son or daughter-in-law, pleasures of having the grandchildren and great grandchildren, and recent medical reports. When I was the activities coordinator, I posted a topic of the week in hopes that it would spur conversations into a positive direction and also would be a theme about which people would write for our literary magazine. Some of these topics can lead to stimulating discussions:

Your first car	Shakespeare	Your parents
Delivery of coal	Learning to swim	Radio programs
The milkman	High-button shoes	Coldest day ever
Ellis Island	Pocket watches	High school prom
Streetcars	First time voting	Your hero
Movie stars	Honoring veterans	Lullabies
Best president	White gloves	Paying income tax
Prettiest sunset	Wedding day	Fireflies
Holiday memories	Starting school	Your best vacation
Social Security	The Superbowl	Beloved pet

So now you know of some topics you can use to start conversations. The next issue is getting involved in activities and in trips. If your building does not have an activities coordinator, try to organize a resident committee or a committee of family members to develop an events calendar. During my seven years of planning the activities for Filbert Gardens, I learned to listen to all suggestions and try almost anything once. You really cannot be sure what people will like and what they will hate. One man came furiously to my office after we had a speaker on Japan, explaining that he fought in the war against the Japanese and he did not want to hear about them. Once a woman started to choke me, because the night we had scheduled to go to hear a concert, she was busy. Then there are people on the pleasant end of the spectrum. One woman really wanted to go on one of our trips to a rehearsal of the symphony orchestra, but the timing, which was out of our control, conflicted with her appointment to get a flu shot. I arranged for someone to drive her to and from the doctor's office, so that she would make it back in time to leave for the symphony. I heard her retell this story to newcomers to the building, at special events celebrating the anniversaries of the building, and at my decade of employment celebration. I did not realize how much the arrangements meant to her. I just made them to help her attend an event that was important to her.

Range of Activities

An activities coordinator should schedule for most tastes and interests. The calendar should revolve around holidays and mental and physical activities that are stimulating and age-appropriate. There should also be intergenerational programs to inject the young into your setting, and events where the audience members can participate at various levels. The sound system should be up-to-date, so that people can hear. When a speaker says he does not need to use a microphone because his voice carries, I would always say that his voice may carry, but in order for some people to hear it, it must be amplified. We did not have a large meeting room at Filbert Gardens, so we used the dining room when we expected a big turnout. That fact meant that we could not start those evening programs until the second seating for dinner was finished. This timing issue made some people unable to come, because starting at 8:15 meant that some were already getting ready for bed or had to take medications then or would miss a certain television show. You offer. They can come or not.

We also did not have much of a budget to pay for speakers or entertainment, so I had to ask people to volunteer their time and services. The solution to getting the good acts was to plan far enough in advance, especially for times like New Year's Eve. We also did not own a bus, so when we needed one, we rented it or used a discounted rate negotiated with the bus service from the local agency.

I was able to help several businesses get started by scheduling them to come to our building. One was a clothing line for seniors that had easy fasteners and wider arm holes. A family member suggested that she bring in a box of greeting cards to sell at a discount for residents who could not get to a store so easily. That was a great idea, and soon she was bringing in ten boxes once a month.

I tried to get the residents involved with projects like knitting hats and scarves, writing for the literary magazine, participating in talent shows and spelling bees, and being interviewed by high schoolers about their life stories. We also enjoyed reading advice column questions, having some in the audience give what they thought the solution should be, and then reading what the advice professional wrote. We had performances of sons, daughters, and grandchildren and their dance schools or their recital colleagues on a regular basis. The point is for the coordinator to be open to ideas and to keep the calendar interesting and full.

My favorite activity at Filbert Gardens was making the sunshine needlepoint. We remodeled a storage area to become an activity room and had a contest to name the room. The winning entry was the Sunroom. The only problem was that it faced north and never really got any direct sun. So I took a five foot by five foot plastic needlepoint canvas and drew on it a replica of a picture one of my young daughters had drawn, a sun with a smiling face and sunglasses. Emanating from the sun was a rainbow. I took it to every resident and had him or her make a needlepoint stitch on it. The rest I filled in myself. We had it framed and hung it on the new wall in the Sunroom, complete with a small plaque that commemorated each resident's participation. These many years later, it still shines rays of happiness on all who use the room.

Being Part of the Community

So when you move into your senior building, your job will be to try the various events. My advice to one disappointed resident can also apply to you at some point: "I am sorry you did not like this particular activity. I hope you like the next one."

On the grounds of Filbert Gardens was a community center that programmed activities from newborns to the elderly. The senior adult department of this award-winning center set aside two days a week for all-day programming for seniors. Our residents either walked over or took the private bus. They could choose from lectures, a political action group for seniors, exercise programs, swimming, workout rooms, a subsidized lunch, and seminars ranging from music and art history to current events. There, they met seniors from various parts of the community, and additional friendships were made. Its dedicated staff left no stone unturned when it came to programming for seniors. If your facility can arrange for you to travel to city and county senior centers, you will have even more stimulating activities from which to choose.

Touching Base with Your Director

You all should feel comfortable speaking to your building director. Whether you have a complaint or a compliment or a question or a concern, you should say what is on your mind. Not everything can be changed to the way you want it, but the director needs to hear from you and should try to meet your needs or tell you why he cannot do something. The director has the balancing job of trying to meet the needs of the residents and their families, following the regulations of the building, keeping the facility safe and clean, supervising the staff, operating within a budget, and both informing and taking direction from the board of directors and management company.

One year, the state organization for homes and services for the aging chose baseball as its convention theme. For the occasion, I wrote a poem which explored the complex job of a building director. The first letter in each line spelled out a salute to that state's home team.

> Greeted in my FIELD with my multifaceted tasks each day,
> Often I ask myself, "Which POSITION should I play?"

> On the PITCHER'S mound, I start the ball
> rolling, or
> Ready always to be the CATCHER with everyone
> throwing me curves, or
> I might be the champion BATTER when I hit one
> out of the park,
> Or I am the designated RUNNER, inspecting my
> building head to toe.
> Leadership, I realize, means being the
> MANAGER to owner and fans.
> Every resident, their families, the board, all form
> my TEAM,
> Spurring me on to do my best in this honorable
> LEAGUE.

In addition to finding a director who is ready to go to bat for you and her staff, you should visit your activities coordinator regularly. When I was the activities coordinator at Filbert Gardens, I wrote this paper for a roundtable discussion at a convention of the National Council on Aging. I have made some changes in the text to fit more appropriately here. It gives you concrete examples of how activities can help people adjust to a senior residence.

"Reinforcing Dignity in a Well-Elderly HUD Residence"

On a recent Sunday afternoon as I was getting ready to leave the house to go to an activity at my senior citizen building, I turned to my husband and said, "I feel that because I had an idea to have this activity, I have changed people's lives briefly today." My husband replied, camera around his neck, holding the hands of our squirming son and two daughters, "You certainly changed MY life for today!"

When I arrived at Filbert Gardens, I saw people dressed in sports jackets and ties and spring dresses. There was a definite, excited hubbub as they congregated near the door to our activity room where we were about to have our building's ten-year celebration. Their lives HAD been changed for that day, however briefly. They had the pleasure of anticipating the event, the getting ready for the day, the enjoying the event itself, and the discussing it afterward.

As their activity coordinator, I respond to the challenge of changing their lives by affording them meaningful ways to spend their time. The caliber of our activities gives our residents a sense of belonging together. Filbert Gardens was started ten years ago. It is a federally subsidized senior citizen apartment for the independent well-elderly. This Housing and Urban Development (HUD) building houses 199 women and 71 men currently. Our average age is 83. Since we are not-for-profit, we have only small subsidies to support our activity program. Even so, we are known for our high standards and community involvement. We have a full monthly calendar of the usual classes, discussion groups, religious services, entertainment, and mental and physical exercises. We program anything from bingo to chamber music, or depending on your point of view, from chamber music to bingo. Since we are located by a neighboring community center, I am fortunate to be able to draw on its recreational resources and its substantial programming.

I would like to share several of my more successful programs with you in the hope that you will go back to your facilities and share with your seniors such activities as: the vacationing on an imagined trip, the publishing of their stories in a literary magazine, the teaching of the National Council on Aging's Memory Course, and the addressing of the needs of the aging in place.

Imagined Vacation—Since many of our residents can no longer travel to far-away places, I take them on a pretend vacation in the middle of each winter. Last year it was Hawaii, and this year was Japan. How do I choose the location? I actually base it on what entertainment I can hire for a low cost. I spend on average $1.00 per person for these vacations. That price includes the souvenirs, the additions to the dinner, and the evening's entertainment.

Setting the mood is the most important first step, because it garners anticipation over the course of several weeks. Through the generosity of the airlines, I use travel posters with vivid scenes of the vacation spot as advertisement during the two weeks before. On the vacation day itself, I schedule an afternoon slide or video program about the location. I find a willing travel agent, airline representative, or fellow traveler, who through his talk, makes us feel as though we are actually in the country we are seeing.

Following the questions and answers in this colorful session, we have our nightly mandatory dinner. I work with the dining room manager in planning the thematically appropriate meal. For Hawaii, we had the serving tables set up in luau fashion. The appetizer was even served in a half shell of a carved-out coconut. For the Japan trip, we offered chopsticks for the teriyaki beef. Residents are encouraged to dress in clothing from our destinations when they come to the dining room. Some wore clothing from trips they had to those sites.

At each place setting, I put a souvenir—a plastic lei for Hawaii and an ornamental fan for Japan. These keepsakes, tangible, yet inexpensive, serve to reinforce the special day long after it has passed. The evening entertainment, in these cases hula dancers and a Japanese dance ensemble, gives a colorful and lively end to a full day.

Residents who had actually traveled to these places have commented on how this activity brought back happy memories, and some, who had never been or who no longer travel, felt as though they were "really there." It is quite a spirit booster, especially when the trip is to a warm location in the middle of the winter. No luggage was lost!

Literary Magazine—When I read the occasional samples of creative writing that were contained in our monthly newsletters, I felt that if I could group them together in a literary magazine, they would have a greater impact. I also felt that this kind of project might appeal to those who do not enjoy group activities. People submitted new material, some of which was inspired by our weekly posted memory-sharing topics. Some writers submitted poems or stories they had written long ago.

After I collected enough for about twenty typed pages, I compiled the magazine. The six steps it takes to ready a magazine form the anagram appropriate for visiting Washington, DC, in the springtime. It is "petl dc"—that is, P-E-T-L-D-C—proofread, edit, type, layout, duplicate, collate.

For the debut of our literary magazine, I scheduled a party. The authors, with flowers on lapels, sat in front facing the audience. I read the introduction to the issue and then called up each contributor in turn. They either read their own selection or had me do it. Each one felt that special sense of recognition as the neighbors applauded the work. They said things like: "I have not felt so proud of what I had written since I was in grade school." "If it had not been for this magazine, my poem would still be stuffed in my drawer." "I was never before applauded for what I did by myself." Even the audience members said that they did not know we had such talented residents here.

The magazine, called *The Mirror*, comes out twice a year. Each new issue contains work by the regulars as well as by first timers. It has become an important reflection of our-dignity-in-aging concept for both its writers and its readers.

NCOA's Memory Course—I have had great success in using the National Council on Aging's (NCOA) Memory Course, published in 1981 and written by Florence Garfunkel and Gertrude Landau. It is an appealing and practical course, because it gives seniors specific ways to help them feel that they are in better control of their memories and to help them fight their fears connected with memory loss. The six-session course philosophy stresses that everyone forgets things, that there are coping mechanisms, and that a most important thing you need to remember about forgetting is your sense of humor. The specific teaching tool my residents found most helpful was the mnemonic device ARC—A-R-C. The "A" stands for association. The "R" stands for repetition. And the "C" stands for concentration. The homework was to use association, repetition, and concentration to help stimulate the memory. Each week, we would share our successes and give suggestions to cope with our problems.

This memory course reinforces the students' dignity, because it emphasizes that the person is not alone, that he should keep his sense of humor, that she may have a strategy that could help someone else, and that there are still many more things remembered than forgotten. A graphic example the authors suggest is in dealing with a shopping list. If you put your items on a random list, you may or may not remember what to get when you are at a certain aisle in the market. But if you organize your list into categories, you have a better chance of buying all that you need.

During the six sessions, my seniors were pleased that they could discuss their memory problems with each other, that they could share some helpful coping mechanisms, and that they could even remember when the class met.

Programs for Aging in Place—The final area I would like to discuss is programming for those who are aging in place. Certainly, our populations are growing older. Since Filbert Gardens opened, our average age has increased by nine years. Although I have many residents who continue to recreate outside of the building, I do have a growing number who need stimulation in-house. The three important points to keep in mind as we program for our aging seniors are 1) to bring the world to your facility without lowering your presentation level, 2) when planning an event, inform your speakers of the wide experience and knowledge base of your population, and 3) that if concessions need to be made for aging, they should be for length of program rather than for content.

To help meet the needs of my more frail residents, I

began a weekly activity called the In-House Group. Over the last year-and-a-half, we have solved most of the President's problems and have pinpointed solutions to many foreign trouble spots. Our high level, lively discussions have two rules: everyone must speak, and anyone may disagree. We balance the discussion with not only the cognitive expression of what did happen in the news, but also with the sharing of our feelings about what happened. This raises the discussion level into the affective domain, validating the participants' feelings. When I look around the room during the sessions, I see that most of my members, with their canes and walkers, would still be by themselves in their apartments were it not for such an accessible group. I personally call them my Canes and Ables.

To help my general residents better cope with aging in place, I try to bring the world in to them, emphasizing what they can do. Some activities which have boosted their self-esteem are as follows:

We had a spring dance recently. It was advertised as "Swing into spring by coming to our dance. Tap your toes or your cane. Even dance to the sounds of the Swing Era." We had over 120 in attendance or should we say attend-dance.

Another activity was our fashion show where the residents were the models. They seemed to walk even taller when they were marching down the runway.

At our talent show, we found out that some residents

could kick higher or sing better than they thought they could.

An excellent activity for emphasizing the dignity of our senior citizens was the birthday party when our first resident turned 100 years old. His speech recounted the highlights of his life. And he ended by saying that what is most important to him at this time is keeping active. He even apologized for not being as active now as he was when he was 95 years old.

These projects I have described are but a few examples of meaningful activities in which seniors can engage and which you should have wherever you live. Each time someone participates in a debate with a speaker or dances to a nostalgic tune or writes his life-long philosophy or innermost hopes, he reinforces his personal dignity, and he debunks the myths of negative aging. The investment of an activity coordinator's time is compounded in the senior citizen's interest, anticipation, excitement, and participation. We are perpetual boosters of their self-esteem, raising their level of dignity as befits them.

Keys for Seniors:
- You can be as active or passive as you want, but try everything.
- Make suggestions for activities, lectures, entertainment, and trips into the community.
- Ask your family members if they can perform or participate in an activity.

- Plan for a family vacation.
- Go to surrounding places like community centers and concert halls.
- You will find a whole spectrum of characters in your new facility.
- If you lose something in your purse, check inside the lining.
- The staff should listen to your concerns.
- Take part in the Residents Association and other building committees.
- Use the icebreakers to start stimulating discussions.

Keys for Adult Children:

- Ask for the activities calendar to be sent to you or arrange to have it available online.
- Remind your parent to participate in the activities or to go on the trips.
- Ask your parent afterwards about the activity.
- Attend the programs of interest to you, and bring other family members, especially to the intergenerational ones.
- Volunteer yourself or your children for an activity or a performance.
- Use the staff as authority figures to help your parent follow the facility's rules.
- Understand the impact on your parent of having to give up driving and cooking.
- Use the icebreaker topics to start stimulating discussions.

Chapter 9
Conclusion

Is This Your Last Address?

So now that you have modified your current home to extend your living there or have moved to another kind of senior housing, there is one more nagging question. Is this your last address? Only time will give us that answer. With the progress in medicine keeping us healthier and able to live longer, our need for a higher level of care may be postponed, but it will probably come at some point. I am always intrigued by the studies that say your odds of getting cancer are reduced by 50 percent if you eat this sort of green vegetable or take this supplement. If you add up the percentages of all the good things you put in your body or do for your body, you may have a 900 percent chance to live longer! Additionally, if you take something like fish oil, you may be able to have a keener mind to go with that better body. The point is you cannot really predict how much living there will be ahead of you. You can only try to do your best to assess your living situation and make sure it is the right one for you at each stage of this time of your life. If you are going to succeed in senior living, you should reside in a place that provides you comfort, safety, and happiness. If you are not there now, I wish that you would do things to get yourself to that place. Use these informational keys to open up a new outlook for yourself. If either you or another relative is locked out of the family's inner circle, now is the time to unlock that door. Otherwise, you are wasting time and energy, both of which are diminishing.

To the adult children, remember that another form of a key is a combination lock. I hope that by following these ideas, you will now have the right combination of patience, creativity, and support to help your parent through this important time.

Future Possibilities

It is also interesting to think about what the future will hold for senior housing. I envision investors of conglomerates buying up properties or building new ones. They will make sure these places have a coffee house atmosphere like a Starbucks, maybe called SeniorBucks. There certainly will be a modified gym, plush bedding, and an internet café area. However, I think that the way we use a keyboard will have to be changed. Because of our arthritic fingers and the possibility of continued injury from repetitive motions, perhaps we should work our keyboard using our feet. That way, we would get aerobic exercise benefits at the same time we are emailing our family and friends. Maybe the walls of the structure will be insulated with all the plastic water bottles we have discarded. Perhaps, we can view our rooms or apartments through virtual reality glasses that display our beloved family home instead of the current walls, so even though we now live in a place that gives us a higher level of care, it would look to us as though we have stayed in our former home. The most sought after places, whether we are very poor or very rich or in between, should promise to take care of all of our financial management, including our dealings with Medicare and drug insurance companies. These features would certainly help to bring in residents. Even though aging leads to loss of mental and physical properties and of loved ones, we can still vow to live our last years in comfort.

Final Thoughts

On my last day as the director of Filbert Gardens, when it was time for me to change careers, I thanked my residents, their families, their aides and companions, the staff, the board of directors, and the management company. It is the working together of these groups that makes for a well-run senior building. I ended my thanks with these thoughts:

Because of the mission of Filbert Gardens, you are able to live in your own apartment yet be close to your family. I once heard an idea attributed to Mother Theresa, that in India, the disease is poverty, but in America, the disease is loneliness. We here at Filbert Gardens have found the cure for loneliness. Whenever you are having a sad day, you can always talk to a neighbor or look out the window to remind yourselves how lucky you are to be here. It reminds me of a joke about the man who got a new dog. He excitedly invited over his neighbor to show off how smart the dog was. The dog ran in, stared at his master, tail wagging furiously, mouth open in a smile, eyes bright with anticipation. The man pointed to the newspaper on the couch and commanded, "Fetch!" Immediately, the dog sat down, the tail wagging stopped, and the smile disappeared. He hung his head, looked at his master, and said in a whiney voice, "My tail hurts from wagging so much, and that dog food you have been feeding me tastes absolutely terrible. Also, I cannot remember the last time you took me out for a walk." The neighbor looked puzzled. "Oh," explained the dog owner, "he thought I said, 'Kvetch'!"

I would remind you that if you feel like kvetching (Yiddish for complaining), try fetching—as in volunteering, helping a neighbor, going for a walk, attending an activity. In closing, I certainly want to thank my family for their loving support. I am honored that my husband and parents are here today. I have tried to keep Filbert Gardens as superior as it was when I was handed its keys. Now as I return the keys, I am reminded of what it says in Leviticus 19:32: "You shall rise before the gray-haired, and you shall grant glory to the face of the old." The poet,

Danny Siegel, has interpreted that phrase to mean that you will make the faces of your elders shine. I hope that I have helped to make your faces shine. Thank you for granting me that privilege.

I then turned in my keys to the office staff, including the master key to all the apartments. I now hope that by reading this book you will be able to use some of the informational keys I have explained to help you in your years in senior living or to help your parent during this challenging period. Turn your kvetch into fetch. Do something.

Chapter 10
Resources

As I said at the beginning of the book, none of us is truly independent. The sheer length of this list proves that it really is not easy to age without the help from some resources. Whatever help you take or give, whatever living environment you choose, may you be comfortable and satisfied.

Disclaimer: These resources are listed as a help to you and do not imply any endorsement of the listed organizations, companies, products, or services. Be sure you check references and research the organizations and companies before you proceed with any of them.

RESOURCES LISTED BY TOPIC

Accreditation:
Council on Accreditation, works with organizations worldwide in developing, applying, and promoting accreditation standards, helping to improve your housing.
   212-797-3000
   www.coanet.org

Continuing Care Accreditation Commission, part of the Commission on Accreditation of Rehabilitative Facilities, is one organization that certifies CCRCs and adult day care.
   866-888-1122
   www.carf.org

The Joint Commission, which used to be called the Joint Commission on Accreditation of Healthcare Organizations (JCAHO), evaluates medical organizations like nursing homes and hospices.
   630-792-5000
   www.jointcommission.org

Aging:
Center for Excellence in Aging Services (with a link to the OASIS Program), a research center that develops, tests, and implements practices and policies that address the needs of seniors, their families, and caregivers.
   518-442-3360
   www.albany.edu/aging

Certified Aging-In-Place Specialists (CAPS), within the National Association of Home Builders, can suggest home modifications, common remodeling projects, and solutions to common barriers.
   800-368-5242
   www.nahb.org/directory.aspx?directoryID=188

National Aging in Place Council (NAIPC), promotes aging in place by working with businesses, organizations, and seniors to be proactive in planning for future needs.
202-939-1745
www.naipc.org

National Council on Aging (NCOA), advocates for older Americans in areas of health and benefits.
202-479-1200
www.ncoa.org   www.benefitscheckup.org

Aids:
American Hearing Aid Associates, represents professionals who can diagnose and treat hearing loss.
800-984-3272
www.ahaanet.com

Catalogs of senior healthcare items like amplified phones, pill organizers, zipper pulls, and foldable canes. Some examples:
Dr. Leonard's
800-785-0880
www.drleonards.com

Taylor Gifts
800-829-1133
www.taylorgifts.com

Gold Violin
877-648-8400
www.goldviolin.com

EyeCare America, a program of the Foundation of the American Academy of Ophthalmology, teaches about eye problems, sight protection, and access to care.
877-887-6327
www.eyecareamerica.org

Alzheimer's Disease:
Alzheimer's Association, voluntary health organization in Alzheimer care, support, and research.
800-272-3900
www.alz.org

Alzheimer's Disease Education and Referral Center (ADEAR), National Institute on Aging (NIA), National Institutes of Health, HHS, helps you find current, comprehensive Alzheimer's disease information and resources.
800-438-4380
www.alzheimers.nia.nih.gov

Alzheimer's Disease Information, National Institute of Mental Health (NIMH), National Institutes of Health, HHS, conducts research on mind, brain, and behavior.
866-615-6464
www.nimh.nih.gov

Alzheimer's Disease Information, National Institute of Neurological Disorders and Stroke (NINDS), National Institutes of Health, HHS, conducts research on neurological disorders and stroke.
  800-352-9424
  www.ninds.nih.gov

Alzheimer's Foundation of America, provides care and services through member organizations to individuals confronting dementia, their caregivers, and families.
  866-232-8484
  www.alzfdn.org

Project Lifesaver International, for wandering Alzheimer patient safety.
  877-580-5433
  www.projectlifesaver.org

Associations:
American Association of Homes and Services for the Aging (AAHSA), a membership of not-for-profit organizations, advocating for standards and services in senior housing.
  202-783-2242
  www.aahsa.org

American Speech-Language-Hearing Association, helps people with speech, language, and hearing disorders receive services and find an audiologist.
  800-638-8255
  www.asha.org/public

Assisted Living Federation of America, advocates for informed choice, quality care, and accessibility in assisted living.
   703-894-1805
   www.alfa.org

Asian American Senior Citizen Service Center, promotes the awareness of the needs of the Asian American elderly.
   714-560-8877
   www.aascsc.org

Center for Excellence in Assisted Living, a group of national organizations dedicated to promoting high quality assisted living.
   202-465-1893
   www.theceal.org

Community Transportation Association of America, interested in transportation planning and coordination.
   800-891-0590
   www.ctaa.org/ntrc/senior

National Adult Day Care Association, provides information, advocacy, and educational opportunities for adult day care.
   800-558-5301
   www.nadsa.org

National Association of Area Agencies on Aging, provides services which make it possible for older individuals to remain in their home.
202-872-0888
www.n4a.org

National Center for Assisted Living (NCAL), the assisted living voice of the American Health Care Association (AHCA), deals with regulatory issues and consumer education.
202-842-4444
www.ncal.org

National Association for Hispanic Elderly, serves the needs of the Hispanic elderly.
626-564-1988
www.anppm.org

National Caucus and Center on Black Aged, addresses the needs of African American elderly, including senior housing.
202-637-8400
www.ncba-aged.org

Caregiving:
Catholic Health Care, provides information on caregiving, senior housing, and health care.
202-296-3993
www.chausa.org/Pub/MainNav/ourcommitments/ElderCare

Eldercare Locator, provides resources for older adults from the U.S. Department of Health and Human Services, Administration on Aging.
   800-677-1116
   www.eldercare.gov

Elder Support Network, part of the Association of Jewish Family and Children's Agencies (AJFCA), which provides information about elderly services.
   800-634-7346
   www.ajfca.org

Family Caregiver Alliance, addresses the needs of families and friends providing long-term care at home. They provide a "Handbook for Long-Distance Caregivers."
   800-445-8106
   www.caregiver.org

National Alliance for Caregiving, provides support to family caregivers and professionals.
   301-718-8444
   www.caregiving.org

National Association of Professional Geriatric Care Managers (NAPGCM), provides a directory of geriatric care managers.
   520-881-8008
   www.caremanager.org

National Family Caregivers Association, educates, supports, and empowers those who care for loved ones.
   800-896-3650
   www.nfcacares.org

Parent Services, Inc., provides care for elderly in Florida.
   800-743-1818
   www.parentservicesinc.com

Red Cross Family Caregiving, provides caregiving classes and a reference guide.
   800-733-2767
   www.redcross.org/services/hss/care/family.html

Elder Abuse:
National Center on Elder Abuse (NCEA), insures the safety and well-being of seniors who are in danger. States have Adult Protective Services divisions.
   202-898-2586
   www.elderabusecenter.org

Elder Law:
American Bar Association, provides research, education, advocacy, and lawyer referral.
   202-662-1000
   www.abanet.org/aging

Expert Law, has online legal help and documents.
  734-665-3493
  www.expertlaw.com

Find Law, provides legal assistance and documents.
  800-455-4565
  www.findlaw.com
  www.public.findlaw.com/elder

National Academy of Elder Law Attorneys, Inc., provides legal advocacy, guidance, and services for the elderly.
  520-881-4005
  www.naela.org

Emergency Alert Systems:
Examples of emergency monitoring systems:
  Life Alert
  800-360-0329
  www.lifealert.com/index.html

  Lifeline Systems
  800-635-6156
  www.lifelinesystems.com

Vial of Life, provides forms for medical and emergency contact information you place on your refrigerator front.
  888-473-2800
  www.vialoflife.com

Geriatrics:
American Geriatrics Society, an organization of health care professionals, dedicated to improving the health, independence, and quality of life for older people.
 212-308-1414
 www.americangeriatrics.org

Government Agencies and Programs (some are listed in others sections of the Resources):
Administration on Aging, a group of area agencies on aging provided through HHS.
 202-619-0724
 www.aoa.gov

Americans with Disabilities Act (ADA) from the U.S. Department of Justice (DOJ), provides information and technical assistance regarding the ADA requirements.
 800-514-0301
 www.usdoj.gov/crt/ada

Congregate Housing Services Program (CHSP), a housing program sponsored by HUD.
 800-245-2691
 www.hud.gov/offices/hsg/mfh/progdesc/chsp.cfm

HIPAA Information, answers questions about the standards for the privacy of health information, according to the Health Insurance Portability and Accountability Act of 1996.
   800-368-1019
   www.hhs.gov/ocr/hipaa

National Institute on Aging (NIA), part of the National Institutes of Health (NIH), conducts research into the nature of aging.
   800-222-2225
   www.nia.nih.gov

U.S. Department of Health and Human Services (HHS), the government's principal agency for protecting the health of all Americans and providing essential human services.
   877-696-6775
   www.hhs.gov/aging

U.S. Department of Housing and Urban Development (HUD), the government's link to housing issues, including community development and access to affordable housing.
   202-708-1112
   www.hud.gov/groups/seniors.cfm

Guides:

Gilbert Guide, Inc., a listing of information on long-term care facilities and services.
   415-668-1532
   www.gilbertguide.com

Guide to Retirement Living, a database of senior housing, assisted living, nursing homes, home health care services, and professional resources in the mid-Atlantic region.
   800-394-9990
   www.GuidetoRetirementLiving.com

Health:

American Medical Association, provides you with basic professional information on licensed physicians.
   800-621-8335
   www.ama-assn.org/go/doctorfinder

Health Information, provides information and support to manage your health.
   only online
   www.webmd.com

National Institutes of Health (NIH), a part of the U.S. Department of Health and Human Services, conducts and supports medical research.
   301-496-4000
   www.nih.gov

NIH Senior Health, provides health information from the National Institute on Aging (NIA) and the National Library of Medicine at NIH.
   888-346-3656
   www.nihseniorhealth.gov

Health Insurance:
State Health Insurance Assistance Program (SHIP), provides one-on-one counseling and assistance to people with Medicare and their families.
   1-800-Medicare, then ask for health insurance counseling
   www.shiptalk.org

See also the section on Medicare and Medicaid below.

Home Care:
There are many fine companies across the country. These are only two examples.
   Chicagoland Caregivers
   312-633-9005
   www.chicagolandcaregivers.com

   Home Instead
   888-484-5759
   www.homeinstead.com
   www.caregiverstress.com

Hospice:
Hospice Foundation of America, provides leadership in the development and application of hospice and its philosophy of care.
   800-854-3402
   www.hospicefoundation.org

Hospice on internet, provides information and support only over the internet.
   only online
   www.hospicenet.org

National Hospice and Palliative Care Organization (NHPCO), provides support to people and families facing serious illness, death, and grief.
   703-837-1500
   Hotline 800-658-8898
   www.nhpco.org

Information:
Information online, enables you to access business phone numbers.
   411
   www.yellowpages.com

Senior Living, part of the *New York Times* Company, an online information source for aging well.
   212-204-4000
   www.seniorliving.about.com

Long-Term Care:
Consumer Information about Long-Term Care, from the American Health Care Association and the National Center for Assisted Living, provides consumers with information about nursing homes, assisted living, residential care, and other types of long-term care.
  202-842-4444
  www.longtermcareliving.com

Nursing Home Compare, through the Medicare website, provides information about the past performance of every Medicare and Medicaid certified nursing home in the country.
  800-MEDICARE
  www.medicare.gov/nhcompare

Mediation:
Elder Mediation, provides ways for family members to reach agreement.
  www.seniorsapprove.com/mediation.html

Medicare and Medicaid:
Centers for Medicare and Medicaid Services, ensures health care coverage and care for beneficiaries.
  800-MEDICARE (800-633-4227)
  Medicare Fraud and Abuse: 800-HHS-TIPS (800-447-8477)

www.cms.gov (home page for programs and information)

www.cms.gov/PACE (explains the Program of All-Inclusive Care for the Elderly)

www.cms.gov/States (provides specific state Medicaid information)

www.medicare.gov (home page for Medicare information)

www.medicare.gov/contacts/static/allStateContacts.asp (lists State Health Insurance Assistance Program (SHIP) counselors in each state)

www.mymedicare.gov (gives you access to your account)

Medicare Rights Center, provides a source of health care information and assistance for people with Medicare.
202-544-5561
www.medicarerights.org

National Consumer Protection Technical Resource Center (formerly called the Senior Medicare Patrol or SMP), educates and empowers seniors in the prevention of health care fraud and abuse.
877-808-2468
www.smpresource.org

Moving Information:
American Moving and Storage Association (AMSA), sets industry standards and provides consumer information.
703-683-7410
www.moving.org

National Association of Senior Move Managers, provides information about the physical and emotional aspects of relocation for older adults.
877-606-2766
www.nasmm.com

United States Postal Service, offers an official change of address form.
800-275-8777
https://moversguide.usps.com/?referral=USPS

U.S. Department of Transportation's Federal Motor Carrier Safety Administration, offers guidelines for moving, finding a mover, and viewing complaint histories.
888-368-7238
www.protectyourmove.gov

Ombudsman:
National Long-Term Care Ombudsman Resource Center, provides support and training to the Ombudsman programs.
202-332-2275
www.ltcombudsman.org

Reverse Mortgage Information:
Reverse Mortgage Information, provides consumer advice and eligibility requirements.
888-687-2277
www.aarp.org/money/revmort

Senior Services:

AARP (formerly called the American Association of Retired Persons), provides support through this nonprofit, nonpartisan membership organization for people age 50 and over.
  888-687-2277
  www.aarp.org

Gray Panthers, honors maturity as it works for social and economic justice.
  800-280-5362
  www.graypanthers.org

Groceries delivered to your home:
  Peapod.com
  800-573-2763
  www.peapod.com

  WeGoShop.com
  877-934-6746
  www.wegoshop.com

Prepared meals delivered to your home:
  Home Bistro
  800-628-5588
  www.homebistro.com

Meals on Wheels Association of America, an organization representing those who provide meal services to those people in need.
   703-548-5558
   www.mowaa.org

Schwan's Home Service
   888-724-9267
   schwans.com

Senior Service America, Inc., promotes civic involvement and employment for adults, subject to certain age and income restrictions.
   301-578-8900
   www.seniorserviceamerica.org

Social Security:
Social Security Administration, the government agency that manages this economic program.
   800-772-1213
   www.ssa.gov

Supportive Living Facilities:
Supportive Living Facilities (SLF), alternatives in Illinois to nursing home care for low-income older persons under Medicaid.
   217-782-0545
   www.slfillinois.com

Universal Design Principles:

Trace at the University of Wisconsin-Madison, one example of a research organization that makes technologies accessible and usable.

608-262-6966

www.trace.wisc.edu

Vacation Services:

Accessible Journeys, provides travel opportunities for mature travelers, slow walkers, wheelchair travelers, their families, and their friends.

800-846-4537

www.disabilitytravel.com

Elderhostel, provides travel experiences for people age 55 and older.

877-426-8056

www.elderhostel.org

TripNurse, LLC, provides companion nurses for your travels around town or around the world.

303-460-8416

www.tripnurse.com

Your Cruise Concierge, LLC, specializes in multi-generation family reunion cruises.

877-922-2922

www.yourcruiseconcierge.com

Volunteer Opportunities:

ProLiteracy Worldwide, provides information for volunteering to tutor with your local Literacy Council.
  888-528-2224
  www.proliteracy.org

Senior Corps, a program of the Corporation for National and Community Service, provides information about the Retired Senior Volunteer Program (RSVP) and programs for Foster Grandparents and Senior Companions.
  800-424-8867
  www.seniorcorps.gov